be your own boss

A PRACTICAL GUIDE TO ENTREPRENEURSHIP

CP/494

D1077591

This edition published in the UK in 2018 by Icon Books Ltd, Omnibus Business Centre, 39–41 North Road, London N7 9DP

Distributed in Australia and New Zealand by Allen & Unwin Pty Ltd, PO Box 8500, 83 Alexander Street,

41 Sir Lowry Road, Woodstock 7925

ISBN: 978-178578-381-4

Typeset in Avenir by Marie Doherty

Printed and bound in the UK by Clays Ltd, Elcograf S.p.A.

About the authors

Alison Price is a Chartered Psychologist and Occupational Psychologist who has coached senior leaders and CEOs in prestigious organizations. As well as being an inspirational keynote speaker, Alison lectures at Kingston University London and comments within the media on motivation and success. She was a semi-finalist in the competition `Britain's Next Top Coach'.

David Price has spent two decades studying achievement and success. He holds qualifications in coaching, psychology and neurolinguistic programming. He provides advice to entrepreneurs and those starting a business, and has headed a social enterprise that raises funds for charity.

Alison and David are passionate about enabling entrepreneurs to be successful, so get access to free resources at:

www.TheSuccessAgents.com

Authors' note

This book contains frequently used research and methods. Where we know the source we have been sure to reference it, but our apologies here to the originators of any material if we have overlooked them.

Dedication

This book is dedicated to everybody who has had a dream to build something and has gone for it. Some people lead the way while others follow. If you have a passion for your interests, want to live by your values and are committed to putting in the effort towards building an enterprise to achieve these things, then you are most certainly a leader.

A special thank you to Alison's sister, Jacqueline Hardt, who not only read and scrutinized the content of this book, but also acted as our roving researcher in the US and interviewed some of the entrepreneurs we feature.

Contents

Introduction

17 March, 2008 was a life-changing day for us. We were on holiday in Australia, sitting on Bondi Beach, away from the all-absorbing treadmill of our day-to-day schedule working in the financial service industry. This enabled us to take a step back and ask ourselves fundamental questions such as, 'How do we want to spend our waking hours?' and 'If we could do anything in life what would it be?'

On Bondi Beach, our dream to start our own business venture was born – working with organizations and individuals to help them to achieve their goals, through the application of psychology, motivational techniques and consultancy advice. You may have had a similar moment in time when you first 'caught the bug'. We can tell you from experience that it's a great bug to catch.

That day, we had no idea how things would turn out and we had big doubts, as taking a step into the unknown and working for yourself can be a very daunting prospect. Like any business, we certainly still have room to improve and grow, and we continually put effort into this. However, if while sitting on that beach we could have known all of the amazing things that we would achieve in our first five years – not least writing our fourth book, which you are currently reading – we'd have been absolutely stunned.

If you are at the start of your journey as an entrepreneur you probably have some of the same anxieties we did, but you should also feel very excited by the possibilities that lie ahead. Be inspired by the words of the famous inventor, Thomas Edison:

If we did all the things we are capable of doing,
we would literally astound ourselves.

The purpose of this book is to catalyze *you* to astound yourself.

Our take on entrepreneurship

A traditional definition of the word 'entrepreneur' might go something like this:

Entrepreneur: A person who sets up a business or
businesses, taking on financial risks in the hope of profit
Oxford English Dictionary

However, we see this as a somewhat outdated view. Let us explain why.

Firstly, although many entrepreneurs *are* aiming to make money, others have a different primary focus – for example, they are dedicated to tackling a worthy cause that is dear to them. Admittedly, someone like the late Anita Roddick, the founder of the successful retail chain The Body Shop, had to earn money to pay the bills. However, through her work she also challenged the cosmetics industry to reduce cruelty to animals through inhumane testing. Being an entrepreneur isn't always solely about making a profit, and therefore the principles within this book apply more broadly (although you'll find plenty of tips on how to make money contained in the next 25 chapters!).

Secondly, we subscribe to Richard Branson's famous quote that entrepreneurship is about turning what excites you in life into capital, so that you can do more of it and move forward with it. We've met many people who have successfully turned a long-standing hobby into their livelihood and have lost count of the number of times we've heard the phrase, 'Work doesn't feel like work.' The case studies in this book are proof that it is possible to make a good amount of money while doing the things that you love.

Finally, traditional definitions of entrepreneurship often emphasize the element of risk-taking. Clearly, some case studies featured in this book do fit with this school of thought. However, while researching entrepreneurship, particularly among the current generation of entrepreneurs, we've commonly found a very different and far less risky approach to starting a new venture. Advances in technology and communication have made it easier to start a venture from the comfort of your armchair with little more than a laptop, internet connection, some spare time and a bucketload of enthusiasm.

Therefore among modern entrepreneurs we've found a very common pattern – aspiring entrepreneurs frequently have an idea for a new venture and begin to trade without a formal business plan or a bank loan. Their emphasis is on testing the market with very little risk and minimal financial investment. Using this strategy, they hone their niche, research their target market, and critically, this period of 'dabbling' confirms the decision about whether to go ahead or not. The philosophy is very much along the lines of, 'little to lose, everything to gain.'

Obviously there will always be some risk involved when starting a new venture (particularly if you are relying on it to pay the bills), and you need to be sensible when embarking on this type of journey. However, many people take the view that the job market is so unstable these days that working for yourself can actually be a safer bet. At least entrepreneurs are in control of their own destiny, have the power to make decisions to change the course of their venture and know the truth about how it is performing.

Throughout *A Practical Guide to Entrepreneurship*, we'll focus on this alternative, lower risk approach to starting a business or social enterprise. You'll find it particularly helpful if you are looking to start your own venture, large or small. If that is the position you are in then you are the person that we've had in mind as we've written this book and we hope that it gives you a short-cut to success.

A blueprint to your success

An important thing to note is that this is a *practical* guide to entrepreneurship. There are many other books and

4

courses out there that teach you academic and theoretical approaches to starting a business, and you may wish to complement the knowledge gained through this book with information from such sources. However, this guide is deliberately designed so that you can throw the traditional textbook out of the window. Rather than being another book that tells you what you are *meant* to do, this guide covers what successful entrepreneurs *actually do* in the current day and age. With key points covered in each chapter, we'll show you simple but effective strategies that are working for entrepreneurs right now, and will help you to apply them yourself.

To help you to achieve your own ambitions, this book is packed with case studies of real people running a wide range of successful ventures, from a music production studio to a bakery to a cricket bat factory. We describe exactly how these ventures got started and how they grew, giving you a blueprint for success.

Some ventures featured as case studies are relatively new and consist of sole traders; some are well established and employ teams of people; others have successfully been sold on for significant sums of money. This variety is designed to ensure that there is a relevant case study to inspire you, whatever your venture, although many of the lessons are applicable across a range of different businesses. By following each entrepreneur's story throughout the book, you'll soon notice a number of common themes that can show you how to achieve success. Furthermore, if you know that you want to become an entrepreneur, but are at a loss for precisely what to do, you'll find lots of ideas to help get you started.

Good luck with your journey – and enjoy it!

We wish you the very best on your entrepreneurship adventure. It will be challenging, but it will also be a hugely rewarding experience. Revisit this book along your journey and re-learn the lessons that our group of entrepreneurs has shared with you. Most of all, do share with us your own success stories, as we would love to hear them.

Alison & David Price
info@thesuccessagents.com

1. Why become an entrepreneur?

*Everybody else at university talked about getting a
job, but I wanted the freedom, challenge, excitement
and adventure of having my own business.*

Steve Roe, Hoopla

Entrepreneurship is satisfying and addictive. When we interviewed the entrepreneurs (like Steve Roe) for this book we couldn't help but feel the glow of pride and passion that came from them. They have been rewarded with an exciting journey, achieving what they wanted and more. With hindsight, the benefits (and drawbacks) of being an entrepreneur are clearer. But in the face of uncertainty, before their journey began, what made them take the plunge – and what factors could be tempting you right now?

Key push and pull factors

We've interviewed a wide range of entrepreneurs from very diverse backgrounds and industries and have found a surprisingly common answer to this question. Aspiring modern-day entrepreneurs are typically:

1. Fed up with their current existence, feeling:

- Demoralized by a lack of opportunity to progress and achieve their potential.

- Undervalued and underpaid.

- Caught up in the rat race.

- Frustrated by poor management and drained by office politics.

2. Excited by the opportunity to create a better future, where they can:

- Be in control, even in the face of economic uncertainty.

- Anchor work around a personal passion, that doesn't feel like work.

- Live an existence that is in harmony with personal values.

- Have greater flexibility to work when and how they want.

- Feel that life has real meaning – spending precious time doing something that matters.

- Put a strong technical skillset to better use, working for themselves and therefore reaping *all* the benefits of their hard work.

3. At a crossroads where they feel that they have nothing to lose by taking the plunge:

- Being made redundant.

- Being made to reapply for a job they don't actually want.

- Not succeeding at interviews for a new job.

The only sure bet in this world is yourself.

Ryan Prettyman, Radiation Detection Services Inc.

- Which of the above reasons resonate with you?

- Are there any other push and pull factors, specific to your own circumstances?

You can think of push and pull factors as being like a magnet. Once these factors become strong enough, they will force you to move from where you currently are and mobilize you to take action.

Starting the ignition

Using the metaphor of a road journey, you have now found the motivation to get in a car and start the entrepreneurial engine. But what do you do next?

One option is to jump in the car, drive, and see where you end up. This could be fun and might lead you to some amazing discoveries along the way. However, you then risk wasting a lot of time and money and potentially missing out on better opportunities. Worse still, you could end up hating your destination and wishing you'd just stayed at home. In other words, you can end up defeating all of the reasons why you became an entrepreneur in the first place and may find you're in a worse place than you were before.

For this reason, we advocate beginning with the end in mind, and thinking, 'What are the ingredients that make for a successful destination?'

What makes a successful destination?

You might equate a great entrepreneurial destination with a black Amex card, five star hotels and a massive home. But before you leap on the bandwagon and try to make millions, just pause for a moment and ask yourself: 'What is success?'

It's interesting, in the first instance, to consider what society views as success. If an entrepreneur banked, say $1,000,000 in personal income each year, do you think society would label them as a failure?

But the key question we ask is, 'At what cost is that so called "success" achieved?' For some, the toll on health and relationships alone will be immense.

Achievement is certainly an important element of success, and something that aspiring entrepreneurs are hungry for. However, we believe there are two other key factors which are equally worthy of consideration and pursuit, which we advocate you aim to factor in when planning your entrepreneurial venture: Meaning (M) and Positive Emotions (P), which, together with Achievement (A), make up our 'MAP to Success'™. So let's take a look at Meaning and Positive Emotions in more detail.

The 'MAP to Success'

M – Meaning

There's no doubt that being an entrepreneur can be an immensely time-consuming experience. So before you go all guns blazing down the entrepreneurship route, you should stop and realize the value of your life, and reflect on the question, 'What actually matters to me?'

Let's fast forward to the end of your life. Imagine yourself looking back over everything you've done – what would make you say, 'I did something really valuable with my time?' It can be quite sobering to think about this, whether you are an entrepreneur or not.

So what drives 'meaning'? This can be hard to describe and will obviously vary between people, based on personal values. But key ingredients in the 'meaning' recipe often include:

- Deep relationships with others.
- Being part of something bigger than you that positively impacts many people.
- Leaving a legacy.
- Being proud of putting your energy and talents towards something really special or important.
- Experiences in life, such as travelling, or doing something new.

One of the best things about being an entrepreneur is that it is a vehicle for greater freedom and choice over how you spend your time. This gives you two viable options for pursuing meaning:

1. Through your work itself

2. Through having greater flexibility with your time, which will enable you to pursue meaning through non-work-related activities

However, there's a very sober word of wisdom from seasoned entrepreneurs to be heard: don't fall into the trap (which is very real and catches many people) of being so driven to achieve that you forget what actually matters to you. No one wants to end up like Mr Burns in *The Simpsons* – cut-throat and rich, but at the same time hated and lonely.

> *Success to me is not about money or status or fame, it's about finding a livelihood that brings me joy and self-sufficiency and a sense of contributing to the world.*
>
> Anita Roddick, founder of The Body Shop

REMEMBER THIS!!! Ideally you can find meaning through your choice of entrepreneurial venture itself. However – and this is key – if your work isn't intrinsically meaningful enough to satisfy the recipe above, work hard to ensure that your entrepreneurial venture is compatible with other avenues in your life where you *can* find meaning. Always remember to make time for the things that matter in your life – usually your friends, family and health.

Positive emotions

So now let's look at the third ingredient in our 'MAP to Success': positive emotions. Even if you are really achieving in your life and life is very meaningful, what does it mean if you feel miserable, stressed, tired, frustrated, upset – are you really successful?

While it may be unrealistic to aspire to feel positive emotions all of the time, we do think that it is reasonable to aim for your day/week/month/year to be overall net positive. It would be a great outcome if, through your entrepreneurial venture, you can aim to raise your average level of positive emotions.

We also believe that positive emotions on their own are *not enough* to feel fulfilled. You could sit by a pool in the sunshine reading good books for a time, but after a while it's likely you'd feel bored and lacking in purpose. The good life needs to be balanced by achievement and meaning in order to actually feel good, factors that can certainly be met in tandem through the vehicle of entrepreneurship.

If you're happy, that's probably the most important thing.
Everyone probably has their own definition of success,
for me it's happiness. Do I enjoy what I'm doing? Do
I enjoy the people I'm with? Do I enjoy my life?
Michael Dell, founder of Dell computers

So what should I aim for?

Through our work in the field we've come to discover that fulfillment isn't a moment in time – a destination – but the experience of enjoying the journey towards a destination that you deem valuable. In other words, through your entrepreneurial venture, you should aim:

> To experience **positive emotions** while **achieving** milestones linked to **meaningful** goals.

This is the essence of a successful journey and destination.

Let the journey begin ...

In the following chapters we will help you to identify precisely where that destination is (i.e. what your entrepreneurial venture will aim to do) and how to take that journey towards it.

To finish the chapter with a sparkle of inspiration, here's a case study about one venture that is following the 'MAP to Success' and is reaping the rewards for its founders as a result.

Peter Thomond and Richard Raynes, SportInspired (launched 2008)

Peter and Richard met on their first day at university, bonding over a pint of beer after a long day getting acquainted with their new surroundings. As they talked about what had led them to be there together, they discovered a common theme: when they were younger, sport had played a key role in their lives. During times of difficulty at home or at school in their adolescent years, sport (karate and white water kayaking, respectively) had provided them with confidence, discipline and a sense of focus that gave them the strength to overcome that adversity.

Fast forward a decade after that first drink and the pair were still great friends, with Richard working as a teacher and Peter about to go into a leading management consultancy. Then, Richard proposed an idea to Peter based on their shared background: that they attempt to encourage young people in Hackney, London to learn more about sports and get involved with local clubs. It would enable those young people who were disengaged in society and unaware of the opportunities in sport around them to find out what was available, try it out and start to benefit from what sport could give to them.

Richard and Peter reached out to a number of local charities, businesses and sports clubs in Hackney to tell them what they planned. A number of community stakeholders bought in and supported it – the local police even knocked on doors and delivered leaflets to get people to attend! Richard and Peter would go on to create a festival-like environment, with local sports presenting what their clubs offered to local young people.

The event was a success and word of it reached UBS, the Swiss bank. UBS approached Richard and Peter with their own proposal: that as part of the bank's Corporate Social Responsibility ('CSR') and talent development programmes, they would commission Richard and Peter to produce another similar project the following year. Richard and Peter were delighted to find a partner with both the talent and cash to help, and created the SportInspired Community Games.

The success of the Community Games in bringing young people into sport, and engaging corporate sponsors with the community, led to UBS continuing to support the program and referring SportInspired to other businesses with CSR and talent development programs. The subsequent growth in clients coming on board meant that their social project became an enterprise that was a full-time endeavour for Richard and Peter.

So how has this venture tapped into Richard and Peter's own 'MAP to Success'?

Meaning: Sport built Richard and Peter's confidence as children and now they are passing this precious gift on to thousands of young people. They are now planning to expand throughout the UK, focusing on the toughest 10 per cent of communities to help young people improve their confidence and their lives through sport. Richard and Peter's dream to help disenfranchised young people make the most of their lives through sport is becoming a reality.

Achievement: Within just five years, SportInspired has worked with over 35,000 people. They've also been recognized with a variety of awards including one from the Prince of Wales's charity, Business in the Community. But while awards are nice, their real sense of achievement comes from how many kids they can get into sport and the community-building outcomes they deliver.

Positive emotion: in Peter's own words …

You know you're alive when you're running your own enterprise. It's scary, things can go wrong, but you are at the locus of control and that is an exciting place to be. The thing is, I'm following my passions, and it's never a chore.

Peter Thomond, SportInspired

IF YOU REMEMBER ONE THING When you are pulled (or pushed) into deciding to become an entrepreneur, in order to be successful you should aim to experience positive emotions while achieving milestones linked to meaningful goals for your venture. If you can do that you've got an amazing journey ahead of you.

---

2. The emotional roller coaster

Success or failure is all down to you.
It's a roller coaster of a ride.

Andrew Gittins, Proposal Automation

In the last chapter we described the three key ingredients for fulfilment in life as an entrepreneur:

1. Creating a sense of achievement.
2. Using your time meaningfully.
3. Feeling net positive emotion along the way

While this makes a great overall package to aim for – and on balance, your life should be better as a result – it's also important to go into entrepreneurship with your eyes open. It isn't always going to be fun and exciting; you need to be prepared for the inevitable roller coaster of highs and lows along the way.

This chapter therefore explores the emotional ups and downs of entrepreneurship and aims to mentally prepare you for the journey ahead, as well as giving you some inspiration for what it is possible to achieve with a lot of hard work!

Richard Stephenson, The Westminster Challenge (launched 2006)
Richard had been fundraising for charity from the age of eight. When he was climbing Mount

Kilimanjaro in 2005 to raise money for charity he 'caught the bug' to become a social entrepreneur – someone who uses his or her entrepreneurial skills to make a positive difference to society or to a worthy cause. He wanted to make the most of his contacts and help charities that were close to his heart.

Richard's big idea (which would later be known as 'The Westminster Challenge') was to run expeditions, where politicians from all political parties, along with senior figureheads from charities, would work on the same team to reach a common goal. This had the dual benefit of raising money for worthy causes while simultaneously building valuable working relationships between charities and politicians.

It took fourteen months of hard graft before the first expedition was launched. This required:

- Sowing the seeds of the idea with potential expedition members and people who could help Richard to realize the vision.

- Recruiting/leading a team of people and a board of Directors to support Richard with the workload.

- Setting up the infrastructure of the venture, for example being legally recognized as a charitable enterprise – which took three attempts.

- Developing a challenging expedition that would grab television and newspaper headlines and attract high-profile names to join in.

- Converting interest in participating in the trek to actual commitment.

- Raising significant support and funding to get the venture off the ground.

All of this was achieved while Richard continued working in his 'day job'.

After months of hard graft, Richard's vision was realized, in the form of a husky dog sled trip across 100km of the Arctic Circle, with temperatures falling as low as –38°C, and with the added challenge of building and sleeping in igloos! The final team was comprised of senior figures from the charitable and political world, including Nick Clegg, who went on to become Britain's Deputy Prime Minister.

Richard and his team of fourteen participants arrived in Finland and were briefed by the professional expedition organization that would lead them across the ice. The team would face life-threatening temperatures, potential death-trap holes in the ice, and needed to be constantly vigilant for local wildlife in an area frequented by bears and packs of wolves.

 While it can be very exciting to leave your comfort zone, it is also associated with the emotions of stress, fear, discomfort and self-doubt.

During the actual Arctic trek, the team felt a mixture of extreme highs and extreme lows. At times Richard said he was so cold he couldn't feel his body. On one occasion, the crew felt exhausted and wanted to stop and give up, but the expedition leader made it clear that this was impossible and extremely dangerous – they had to keep going, no matter how bad they felt.

During your entrepreneurial journey, there will be occasions when you are in so deep you simply cannot give up, no matter how awful you are feeling. You have to take one step at a time and keep going until you reach a point of safety.

Just at the moment Richard wanted to fall on the ice and die rather than continue, a magical experience happened. The Northern Lights appeared in the sky, and to the exhausted crew it felt like an angelic beacon of hope had appeared to guide them home.

Have faith that in the darkest moments of challenge, something will happen that will give you the energy to keep going. The feeling of achievement in these situations is immense.

I'm convinced that about half of what separates the successful entrepreneurs from the non-successful ones is pure perseverance.

Steve Jobs, co-founder of Apple

How could the Arctic expedition act as a metaphor for your own entrepreneurial venture and the highs and lows you will face?

Richard's case study details a number of practical steps required to realize a vision. Have a go at brainstorming what major milestones you might face in your journey of entrepreneurship. Reflect on the likely highs and lows of these milestones.

Being an entrepreneur is *not* the easy option

Many entrepreneurs will argue that getting their venture off the ground and keeping it afloat is one of the hardest things that they will ever do in their whole life.

Being employed is the easy option. As an 'employee' you have:

- Set hours.

- A regular pay check, which you don't have to invoice for.

- A payroll team that pays without you having to chase extensively and which helps to sort out your taxes.

- A job description, clearly specifying what you are doing.

- Someone telling you the strategy of the organization.

- Backup when you are sick and paid sick leave.

- An IT support helpline.

Aside from the practicalities, being 'employed' also avoids some specific challenges relating to your friends and family:

- An inherent understanding that during working hours you are *working* and therefore it is *not* appropriate to contact you for long social chats (whereas when you are running your own business, people seem to get offended when you say you are too busy to talk or meet).

- An inherent understanding that it is rude to ask about how much you are paid (compared to the fact that people seem to think it is perfectly appropriate to ask entrepreneurs how much they are earning).

- Less pressure from well-meaning people constantly challenging you as to whether you are doing the right thing or not.

Added to these challenges is the fact that in most cases, in order to create a safety net underneath a venture, entrepreneurs will often do their 'day job' while simultaneously trying to grow their business. Some people find doing one full-time role stressful enough!

 Talk to other entrepreneurs about their emotional highs and lows (or read books by well-known entrepreneurs) to mentally prepare yourself for the journey ahead.

Why the 'MAP to Success' matters so much...

Whereas Chapter 1 showcased the positive and exciting side of entrepreneurship, this chapter has explored some of the darker times entrepreneurs can face. It is something that you need to go into with very realistic expectations of the emotional demands you will face – it will be a journey of highs and lows.

- The venture tapped into a huge area of **meaning** for Richard – a passion for raising money for charity. The most touching moment of his journey was when the manager of a charity approached him in tears, thanking him for raising money for her organization. The amount they received was enough to keep them open and continue to work for vulnerable people for another six months.

- Richard is very proud of what the Westminster Challenge **achieved** – for example, raising tens of thousands of pounds for a range of charities, large and small, through the Arctic expedition alone, as well as other great fundraising initiatives, such as a trek along the Great Wall of China.

- However, ultimately, the strain of running the charity with little support, while working simultaneously in a day job, overtook the feelings of **positive emotions** derived from its success. Six years after the charity was launched, Richard took the brave decision to close the venture. He doesn't see this as the end of his charitable endeavours but felt that he needed to focus on his personal and professional life for a few years before embarking on another charitable challenge.

Before you proceed down the road of entrepreneurship, or if you are already on the path and are wondering whether to keep going or not, we cannot emphasize enough the need to balance achievement with meaning and positive emotions. These emotional ingredients, plus the added practicalities of time (to commit to running your venture) and money (to pay your bills) are fundamental to sustaining your enterprise.

This chapter certainly isn't saying *don't* be an entrepreneur – quite the opposite: we think that it is one of the best decisions we have made in our own lives.

Even for Richard, who has closed his venture, the sense of achievement and lasting memories will enrich his life forever. But we *do* advocate going into entrepreneurship with realistic expectations of the emotional demands that you will face, and beginning with the end in mind – striving up front to achieve the balance of meaning, achievement and positive emotions in your life.

If you are still hungry to proceed – and we really hope that you are – then the rest of this book will help you to turn your dreams into reality. Chapters 3 to 7 are designed to help you make massive progress with your venture, while minimizing the emotional strain of jumping in too deep.

 Being an entrepreneur can be something that is hugely exciting. However, you need to have a realistic view of the trials and challenges it will put you through. If you are still hungry to proceed, despite the challenges that lie ahead, read on – it's going to be one hell of a ride but you'll get off the roller coaster and say, 'Wow, that was brilliant!'

---

3. On your own or with a partner?

It is nice on your own, you are 100 per cent in control of your destiny. Only venture forward with a partner if you can absolutely trust them; that if I gave them my bank account number, they would not do anything bad to it. If you don't have that level of trust it will not work.

Ryan Prettyman, Radiation Detection Services Inc.

As you embark upon your entrepreneurship journey you are likely to meet people who want to be your 'business partner', for example because you offer a complementary technical skillset to them. This can seem like an enticing prospect, particularly if your potential partner already has an established network or client base.

In some instances formal partnerships really succeed. However, there are also many instances where it can be a rocky road, which makes it much harder to 'enjoy the journey', and to 'reach the destination'. When formal partnerships break down they sometimes have very sticky endings, which can ruin years of friendship and end up in court.

The decision of whether to work with a business partner or not will have a major impact on your day-to-day life as an entrepreneur. Given how frequently entrepreneurs fall into the wrong relationship, this matter is worthy of very careful consideration.

Let's therefore consider the relative merits of going into business on your own, versus with a partner, and look at how to make partnerships successful if you do choose that route.

Sole control?

When running an enterprise on your own you are 100 per cent in control of your destiny. It's akin to getting into a car and having total freedom to go wherever you want – there is no one to disagree with you or to hold you back.

On the flip side, it can also become a lonely journey, and you have to do all the 'driving' yourself. There's no one to pay for half of the petrol, and no option to take two cars if you need to be in different places at once. Plus, when considering what destination to aim for and the best route to take, you miss out on having a valuable second opinion from someone with an equal interest in success.

Dual control?

Sometimes two heads are better than one, particularly if you have complementary knowledge or skills. One of the key issues for entrepreneurs is that they often have a great *technical* skillset, but that is very different to being capable of running a business. They may be good at making a product, or delivering a service, but if they have to make sales through cold calls, or 'network' at an event, they're suddenly out of their depth. So it can be helpful to have a partner whose strengths can support your weaker areas. Solo entrepreneurs also frequently comment that it would be more fun and there would be a lighter weight of responsibility if they had a partner to work with.

However, using our car analogy again, you can see there can also be many problems when embarking on a shared journey. For example when:

- One person wants to reach the destination more, and as a result does more of the driving, while carrying a 'lazy' passenger.

- One person puts in more 'petrol' than the other, leading to an imbalance in financial interest and how rewards are shared.

- You disagree over where you are headed or how you will get there and get stuck as a result, and end up going nowhere.

- One person is hungry to start the engine and go, whereas the other person is distracted by other things and isn't ready to leave yet.

- You haven't agreed formally where you are going and what route you will take, and then the other person changes their mind and leaves you hanging.

- You start getting along less well as the journey continues, but you're stuck in the car together now, and wish you had a way out!

The jury says ...

When we've asked entrepreneurs whether they'd advise formal partnership or not, on balance, the view has been 'Personally, I wouldn't recommend it.' This opinion has been voiced both by relative newcomers to the entrepreneurship game, as well as owners of more established businesses.

However, there are examples where partnership working is the bedrock of success, as exemplified by the following case study.

Deon Girdhar and Chris Williams, Zay D Entertainment (launched 2006)

We have found that many people start businesses linked to a long held area of passion. But what happens if your area of interest is notoriously impossible to break into? For example, imagine that your fascination with music production had led to you dreaming of making music for famous, international artists.

For Chris 'Zay' Williams and his cousin Deon 'D' Girdhar, this dream came true, all from the humble origins of a business that they launched from their bedrooms. They now run their own state-of-the-art music production studio in London and have written and created chart hits. So how did Chris and Deon turn wishful thinking into reality, and how has a successful business partnership underpinned their success?

Deon originally worked in the banking industry, but had been making music in his bedroom for years as a hobby and had learnt the technology behind creating songs. Chris on the other hand had a complementary skillset to offer – as a musician he understood the theory of music.

Life sometimes has a habit of throwing you opportunities that change the course of your life, and for Deon this occurred when he had the chance to visit a world-renowned recording studio in Stockholm that had produced major records for some of the world's leading artists including Britney Spears, The Backstreet Boys and NSync. At the time of his visit it was working on records for Westlife and Enrique Iglesias. Deon felt completely inspired. He looked at the technology in the studio and the technical ability required to use it, and realized that it wasn't completely out of his grasp.

On his return to London, Deon met with Chris for a curry and they discussed how Chris's attempts to further his career as a music producer were not moving forward as much as he would like. Then Chris said, 'Why don't we give this a go together?' Within six months, Chris and Deon had set up their business.

Even though they were cousins, Chris and Deon created a formal contract from the outset, and a formal plan for their joint venture. The plan included a number of realistic milestones and specific financial targets. It was clear that the cousins had highly compatible values and beliefs, for example, the need to work with the utmost integrity at all times. Over the years, these shared values and beliefs have guided critical decision-making and this has helped to keep the partnership united.

This successful working relationship is also underpinned by a selfless and trusting attitude: they are loyal to each other because they are family; if one of them is sick the other one carries on; when they turn up for work they are always on the same team; they do have issues but they work them out by being objective. Such is the bond between the pair that they have committed that, should either one of them not be able to work, the other would continue the business and support them both.

Deon would recommend working as a partnership, but says that it has to be the right person – someone with whom you can simply turn up to work and get the job done, because your relationship is strong. The cousins have fun every day and love working together because they are best friends and are 100 per cent committed to a shared goal.

During their time in partnership, Chris and Deon have successfully grown their business. They started by helping aspiring recording artists to make demos for record labels. This enabled them to create a catalogue of songs used by established artists, and to begin to earn a living from music production. As the aspiring artists promoted themselves to record labels, they concurrently showcased Zay and D's production skills and songwriting abilities. Over time, Zay and D's calibre as a production team was recognized, and they were invited to collaborate with independent and, later, major record labels working with a number of well-known acts. Their studio has since played host to a diverse range of acclaimed songwriters and artists, from award-winning rapper Blade Brown (MTV Top 10 UK MCs 2012) to international chart-topping boyband Blue. What a great outcome from a decision made between the two of them one night at a curry house!

 Tips for making partnerships work
If you do go down the partnership route, here are some tips to help them to work:

- Know yourself: understand your skills and values; then find a partner with complementary skills and shared values.

- You need to have 100 per cent trust in your partner.

- Consider the best time to bring a partner on board. Some recommend that it has to be a partnership from the outset, otherwise the division of assets becomes difficult.

- Find someone who is just as passionate as you about the business and success.

- Make sure it is someone you like spending time with – you'll see a lot of them.

- Make the relationship formal, and ensure that both parties continuously know where they stand.

 For your business to be a success the people controlling it must share the same values, vision and passion. Unless there is a best friend, family member or acquaintance who can share the dream, work just as hard as you, and bring complementary skills to the venture, then consider having sole control over the destiny of your venture.

4. Working out
what you have to offer

*I had great interest and motivation to explore
what I could offer. The more I explored, the
more I did, the more interesting it got.*

Andy Carley, Response Development Training

Once you've made the decision that you want to be an entrepreneur, there is a critical question to answer: what type of products or services will your venture offer?

For some this will be a relatively easy question to answer. For example, in Chapter 14 we'll introduce a beauty therapist called Beverley, who had been working in the beauty industry for years and decided to offer her existing skillset but on a self-employed rather than employed basis. And in Chapter 23 we'll meet Susan, who spotted a gap in the market for a much-needed product that created a foundation for a very successful business.

But for others, it can be really tough when it comes to deciding what you will actually provide to customers, particularly if you come to establish a venture in an industry that is new to you. This chapter therefore concentrates on helping aspiring entrepreneurs identify their general product or service area.

CASE STUDY

Steve Roe, Hoopla (launched 2005)

Steve had dreamed of being an entrepreneur when he was at university, although he didn't have enough confidence then to pursue that dream. So he took what might be considered as the 'sensible' route and worked for a well-known global organization as a management consultant.

Several years later, Steve was between jobs and sitting on a beach in Malaysia, thinking about how much he hated his career. He wrote a list of what he could do with his life, which included:

- Continue working in management consultancy
- Become a policeman
- Become a politician
- Work in space technology
- Work in drama/TV/films
- Start a business

Excited by some of the prospects on his list, Steve's burning desire to become an entrepreneur won through and he decided to direct his efforts towards starting some kind of venture in the acting industry, as this was a key area of passion. This decision entailed some sacrifice in his life; leaving behind the lucrative world of management consultancy required major financial cutbacks, including selling his car, going out less, and moving back home for two years with his parents (who fortunately were happy to have him home).

Still needing to pay the bills, Steve took temp job after temp job, including working in call centres and as a waiter. Steve then got a part-time contract as a runner for a television production company, allowing him to better explore his options within the acting industry.

Through exploring the sub-fields within the industry, Steve discovered a love of improvised comedy – the kind of stand-up improvisation you would see on the television show, *Whose Line Is It Anyway?* Improvised comedy classes were hugely popular in the United States but were relatively uncommon in the UK. Over time, Steve began to explore the different ways that he could make money from this area, for example, through performing, producing shows and teaching.

Initially Steve tried to pursue all of these different avenues at once, but found that he was spreading himself too thin. With hindsight, he realized it would have been better not to attempt to offer multiple products simultaneously but instead find a niche that worked and really concentrate on that.

Chip away looking for gold, then when you find it, stop looking and just mine it!

Steve Roe, Hoopla

Steve's early seam of 'gold' was drop-in improvised comedy classes, offered by his company 'Hoopla'. He started running classes and was able to generate a small profit from these, so he started another class, then another. He simply kept expanding the same product to different local areas, and the more sessions he offered, the more people came. When he began advertising online, the demand for his sessions was so overwhelming that he had to pull the advert as he couldn't match it.

Steve was then introduced to another 'gold mine' when one of his students asked him to run an improvisation training session at her company, which would bring out employees' creativity and build teamwork at the same time. This opened the door to teaching in a more lucrative setting, which he has since expanded. Steve has also gone on to create a Hoopla improvisation comedy club that features improvisers from around the world, which has been recommended as the best place to see improvised comedy in London by the *Daily Telegraph*, a national newspaper.

Over the last eight years, Hoopla has gone from strength to strength, and long gone are the days when Steve lived with his parents and ran Hoopla part-time. When you talk to Steve about his journey, the passion for his work is evident – he's clearly living his dream – and has a life where he works in alignment with his values. He earns a decent living from something that he really enjoys doing. And the achievement he's most fulfilled by? Reflecting back on his unconfident nineteen-year-old self, and imagining how proud he'd be to see his future: 'If I could have told myself all of the amazing things I would go on to do, I'd never have believed it.'

- If you know that you want to be an entrepreneur but like Steve are uncertain which direction you'd like to take, write a list of all of the possible products/services that you could potentially offer. Use the gold-mining analogy: this process is akin to writing a list of towns where you could mine gold and you are trying to pick one spot on which to concentrate your efforts.

- Once you've selected your 'town' to mine in, start exploring the terrain: brainstorm all of the different ways that you could strike gold. You are aiming to find a seam of gold that you can simply keep mining once you get lucky.

But what if you don't know which 'town' to mine gold in?

Steve sat on a beach and wrote a list of all of the things that he could do, and ultimately chose the area he was most passionate about. But how else can you decide what products/services to offer when there simply isn't a clear choice? Here's an activity to help you to find a way forward.

Grab a pad of sticky notes and brainstorm answers to the following questions, writing each answer on a separate note.

1. What skills/strengths do you have that you could make use of in your venture?

2. Where would you like to be based when you operate your venture (on the road, from leased premises, working from home, etc.)?

3. Are you intending to build a venture that will be sold/handed on, or do you feel that it needs to be centered on your personal skillset?

4. Do you want to build a venture from scratch, or could you look to take over/buy into an existing one?

5. In which market(s) do you want to target your venture? As you answer this, think about the strengths and weaknesses of working with different sectors, for example, private corporate; public sector; educational; local community; charitable; global community (online) etc.

6. Going forward, would you like to work on your own or employ a team of people?

7. Where would you like to live in the future (i.e. do you need a 'portable' venture)?

8. If you are working on a commercial venture:

- Would you prefer high-volume sales with relatively low profit margins, or low-volume sales with relatively high profit margins?

- Are you aiming for regular repeat business from clients, or will you provide products/services that are 'one-off purchases'?

- What sales channels would you like to use (e.g. face-to-face meetings, telephone based or internet driven)?

- Roughly, how much profit do you need to make, in order to satisfy your personal expenses?

9. Think of ventures that give you a pang of envy! What is it about them that makes you feel just that bit jealous?

Having answered the nine questions above, you should now have a pile of sticky notes that reflect your wish list for your future venture. Now prioritize your wish list by sorting your notes into four piles:

- The absolutely 'must have' factors – things that are critical to you

- The 'should have' factors – things that are fairly important

- The 'nice to have' factors – things that you'd like but could live without

- The things you don't really care about too much

Now look at your list of possible ventures from the previous activity in this chapter and see if there are any ideas that match your 'must have' factors and 'should have' factors. Also, now that you know what's important to you, aim to think of other ideas that meet these criteria.

Working out what you want to do can take time, but it's time worth taking to think about what you want from your venture up front, before you take action and make concrete plans.

If you're still stuck

If after lengthy pondering, you still feel totally in the dark about which general area to start your venture in, we recommend two things:

1. Read through the case studies in this book: they will give you ideas for a wide range of businesses. See if any of them provide some inspiration.

2. Open your eyes and ears to the world: you are surrounded by successful ventures that can give you ideas. Talk to people, notice what products and services businesses are providing and do online research to spot interesting opportunities. Eventually you will strike gold.

THINK ABOUT IT

In *A Practical Guide to the Psychology of Success*, our sister book in this series, we posed a question that seems to have really struck a chord with readers. We'll pose this question to you again here as, if you're still unsure of what your venture could entail, your answer to this question could be what unlocks the puzzle for you.

The question that we want you to think about is, 'If money was no object, what would you want to spend your time doing?'

IF YOU REMEMBER ONE THING

Before you embark on your own venture it is important to identify what it is you have to offer as a product or service, and what you want from being an entrepreneur, so that you can set out to achieve both.

5. Finding your niche

There's no point being a 'me too company'. Find something that someone hasn't done and do it. Or try and do something that somebody else is doing and do it much better and differently.

Tricia Topping, TTA Group

Some entrepreneurs know what *general* area to launch their venture in, yet this can cover quite a broad remit. So they then face the puzzle of working out whether their product/ service will be a generalist or a specialist one. For example, if you are a photography business, do you specialize in one area, such as weddings, or do you apply your skillset more broadly by photographing events, objects and taking family shots?

Working out what it is your venture offers and to whom is a vital decision, as it goes right to the core of your venture's identity and basic purpose. This chapter therefore explores the pros and cons of occupying a niche, and since on balance entrepreneurs recommend that you occupy a niche, we describe how to find a good one. It also explores how you can hook people using a niche even if you do want to have a more generalist offering behind that.

Why you want a niche offering

There are a number of advantages to your venture occupying a niche:

- It's much easier to describe what your venture does, because what it does is specific.

- It makes it simpler to define who your venture's target audience/market is and you can use a much more focused marketing strategy as a result.

- If your venture's specialism is fairly unique, you face low competition and your product/service may be less price sensitive.

- Your venture can become the best at what it does because it is so specialized.

- You and your venture can become well-known in your industry.

For these reasons, many entrepreneurs from our research sample have recommended finding a niche for your business to occupy.

It's important having a niche because you carve out your identity in the industry. You have to create an identity for yourself to be successful.
Deon Girdhar, Zay D Entertainment

Limitations of a niche
However, successful entrepreneurs have also been realistic as to the downsides of targeting a niche. Having a single niche is equivalent to putting all of your eggs in one basket.

Industry demand can crash (sometimes overnight) and if your venture depends upon that industry, it can face deep trouble without warning.

A further problem with a really specific niche is that your customer base may be smaller, because fewer people want your product/service. Some entrepreneurs have argued that this can actually make marketing very hard and costly, as you have to try harder to reach the limited number of people who might need you.

Also, you may be able to deliver more products or services than the one thing your niche allows for. If you can fulfil requests outside of your 'scope' then why turn them down? Offering a diverse range of products/services has the potential to make life much more interesting than offering the same thing over and over again.

The perceived wisdom is to find a niche. However, if I'd done that I wouldn't be in business. The diversity of scale and scope of my business has allowed me to carry on during difficult times.

Andy Carley, Response Development Training

- Review the advantages and disadvantages listed above, thinking specifically about your chosen business area.

- Which model, specialist or generalist, will work best for you?

How to take advantage of being both a specialist and a generalist

Although, on balance, our research has concluded that having a niche is a good idea, some entrepreneurs are driven or choose to have a more generalist offering. However, we've identified an interesting approach to entrepreneurship that capitalizes on the benefits of both a niche and a more generalist approach, which the following case study illustrates.

Anna Hodgson, The Eternal Maker (launched 2007)

How many entrepreneurs would love to be at a trade show and have a queue of people outside their booth from morning until night, waiting to see their products? For Anna Hodgson this is a reality when she demonstrates her stunning selection of unique Japanese fabrics.

Anna has a talent for spotting trending products that aren't yet available in her home country. She spends hours trawling the internet for new products to import. For example, she'll study Japanese craft blogs, and while she may not be able to read a word of Japanese, she can certainly see the pictures and discover what's 'hot' in that market.

Once she's unearthed a potential gem, she then devotes time to the painstaking process of tracking down the manufacturer of a particular fabric, enabling her to import and sell it. But it's well worth her effort – the Japanese fabrics that Anna has discovered have become one of her biggest selling ranges, and she's become renowned as the supplier of choice when you want to purchase an elusive Japanese textile.

Anna recommends having a niche, especially in retail, because it is very helpful to be known as a specialist. She's been told by visitors at trade shows that they came to the event specifically to see her products after having seen her adverts in trade magazines, online, or through meeting her at previous exhibitions. Her unique products have also attracted nationwide retailers at trade shows, who she now supplies to.

And here's the clever part: Anna has a niche to hook customers in. By offering something different she has a product that attracts a specialist following to her business. However, her business offers a product range wider than the niche that it is renowned for, and sells a selection of typical haberdashery products such as ribbons, buttons and other fabrics. This means that Anna attracts customers who want a specialist product, who then go on to purchase more generally available items from her as well, because she has built a relationship with them.

Anna has struck a great balance between finding a niche and also supplying general products to customers that they could get from many other suppliers, but who then choose to purchase from her. She's found the best of both worlds.

THINK ABOUT IT What's your 'Japanese fabric' – something that you can attract customers with, who can then access your further range of products and services?

USEFUL TIP

How else can you be a niche supplier?

Aside from offering a specialist product or service, there are four other ways that your venture can find a niche:

1. **Price:** You can have a similar product to other enterprises and compete on the basis of cost, where you undercut their prices and attract their customers to you. This has the advantage of operating in a market where demand has been proven. Can you provide 95 per cent of the standard quality, for a significantly lower cost?

2. **Quality:** You can also differentiate yourself by offering a product that is a substantial improvement on the norm, with charges that reflect that quality. Can you improve a standard product to make it highly attractive to a premium market?

3. **Service:** In a world where convenience and comfort is king, you can also find a niche offering exactly what your competitors provide, but delivering in a way that differentiates you and attracts customers. Can you

improve the experience of customers so that they value your services more?

4. **Location:** You can take a tried and tested business model and import it to an area with a potential market to tap, which currently has low competition. Can you provide a product or service that has poor supply locally?

How can you personally use the principles of price, quality, service or location to find a niche?

Know the market

If you do choose to go down the niche route, it's invaluable to know your market before you spend time and money chasing the wrong dream. The next chapter will help you to learn about and test the market before committing 100 per cent to your chosen area, to help you understand the viability of your proposed venture.

Having a niche enables your venture to define itself and its purpose to your customers. However, having a single niche is potentially risky and it may be better to widen what your venture can provide its customers through complementary products and services.

---

6. Researching and testing the market

There was a need for what I could do but not necessarily the demand, so I had to find that. I phoned around my former clients and asked them, if I were to offer my services, would they be interested. When they said yes I knew I could make it work.

Andrew Gittins, Proposal Automation

While conducting our research we've noticed that entrepreneurs aren't typically following the traditional approach to start-up: doing market research, writing a business plan, securing funding, building the infrastructure and beginning to trade.

In contrast, once aspiring entrepreneurs have chosen their product or service area, many 'test' the market. They skip the desktop research stage and begin trading on a very small scale. In other words their 'test' is their market research. This alternative approach can be undertaken with little or no risk, while retaining the comfort blanket of employment in an existing role.

Why test the market?
Let's imagine that you have dreams of running your own retail outlet. You could make the decision to go for it, work hard to obtain funding, find and convert suitable premises, buy all of the required equipment and then open the doors

of your shop – only to discover that there is zero demand for your products. If you've quit your job to make this happen, and you have gone into a significant debt in the process, this can be a terrifying and upsetting position to be in.

Let's contrast this approach with the clever one described below taken by Kate and Richard, who tested out the market first in order to understand the viability of baking for a living.

Kate Smith and Richard Copsey, Holtwhites Bakery (launched 2011)

Richard and his wife Kate were both employed; however, Richard was not enjoying his profession as a teacher as much as he used to. He therefore began pondering the idea of doing something he loved for a living – baking.

Although Richard had been baking in his own kitchen for years, he realized this was very different to baking professionally. So he decided to undertake work experience at a bakery during the school holidays, to see what professional baking entailed, and to learn the ropes.

Richard enjoyed the experience and was keen to test out his new expertise, so he asked ten local friends if they'd each be willing to buy a loaf of bread from him every Saturday. These friends had already sampled his cooking and were more than happy to accept his offer! This gave Richard the confidence to buy the basic professional equipment required to bake on a semi-professional basis (thereby beginning to trade with a very low risk investment).

Word of mouth quickly spread, helped by stalls of tasty products served at local school and church functions. And here's the best part: within just a few months, Kate and Richard had a queue of 60 customers outside their door every Saturday to pick up their weekly order of bread! Demand had become so great that the couple had to say no to new customers – the demand was totally outstripping the amount of bread they could supply from their home.

The couple's confidence had grown immensely and Kate had become hooked on the idea too. They began to believe that, despite having a mortgage to pay and two young children to support, there was potentially a viable business in local artisan baking. Kate and Richard could project sales based on scaling up their current business and had confidence that the income they could generate could balance their personal and business expenses, despite the significant investment in infrastructure and staffing costs that they would need to commit to.

Over time the dream to open an artisan bakery in their local town became more and more enticing and began to take a concrete form. The couple decided to spend their ten-year wedding anniversary in Paris, sampling the best Parisian bread, researching the tastiest deli products, and soaking in the ambiance, to inspire their new venture.

They then got a fortunate break when Kate's brother generously offered them a sum of money to transfer their home baking business to a local retail outlet. As fate would have it, there was a vacant premises on the high street near to their house. With the 'pilot' baking period under their belts, the couple decided to take the plunge, committing to the premises, creating a limited company and buying the professional equipment required for the business. But critically, Kate and Richard had already proved there was demand for their products, they had explored marketing options that converted into customers and they already had a hungry customer base.

Richard handed in his notice to his employer and began the conversion of the premises to a bakery. Prior to opening, Kate also handed in her notice, which freed her up to manage the front of house and its staff, do the book-keeping and bake cakes as well as serve customers in the bakery's shop.

On opening day, the couple reaped yet another benefit of trialling their product – they had a queue of customers outside their bakery who were eager to sample their delicious products. Many of the original 60 clientele from the home bakery phase are still loyal customers to this day.

A year and a half after Holtwhites opened their doors, we sat in the bakery with Kate and Richard, surrounded by hundreds of baking tins, massive ovens and bags of top quality flour. The pride and joy experienced by the couple in their venture is visible on their faces. They now employ eleven staff and have an established retail following as well as providing wholesale to other businesses in the local area.

They've recorded more than double their original sales projections and their achievement has been recognized nationally by the *Telegraph Magazine*, which named Holtwhites Bakery as runner-up in the 'Best Small Shop for Food' award in 2012. It just goes to show where a week's work experience and a trial venture can lead.

How could you use the approach taken in this case study to reduce the risk associated with launching your venture?

Test the market to understand your venture's viability before reaching a point of no return. This can be done with little or no risk.

Other ways to test the market

Many entrepreneurs that we met were originally working within organizations with a similar remit to their proposed venture. This enabled them to understand the market, to explore its products and services, and, importantly, to identify what clients are looking for while being employed. This approach grew their credibility, experience and network within the industry and meant that, when they were ready to take the plunge with their own venture, people were already coming to them with business.

A more traditional approach to market research ...

Here are some other complementary strategies that our entrepreneurs have used, typically alongside a 'test' of the market. They have:

- Spoken to other people who were already doing what they wanted to do. For example a person/organization who offers similar services but in a non-competing local area. This enabled them to gain valuable insight into what works and what doesn't.

- Searched competitors online to find out what they sell, how much they charge and how they market themselves. They didn't just confine the search to the country in which they lived – they looked at what was trending overseas and reflected on whether they could bring a popular trend to their home country.

- Spoken to potential customers to find out whether there is an appetite for their proposed products/services. This had the advantage of generating sales leads, prior to official launch.

- Read published research on their proposed market area.

- Identified direct competitors and approached them to explore possible opportunities to collaborate.

Think of all the people you know and try to identify at least one successful entrepreneur, ideally with a similar business model to the one you want. Contact them to ask them how they tested and researched their market.

What do I want to find out when researching and testing the market?

There are several key things that you need to identify during this research and testing phase, for example:

- Are the products/services that you would like to provide in demand? If so, who is the target market?

- What are your minimum start-up costs to test the market, and can you afford this investment with acceptable risk?

- How much can you sell the products/services for? (i.e. the sale price per unit)

- How many unit sales do you need to make in order to cover personal and business costs?

- Are there any legal considerations that you need to contemplate, prior to testing the market? (i.e. Kate and Richard called round an environmental health officer to their home, to ensure that they complied legally with professional food hygiene standards).

Remember that researching and testing the market has the added advantage of giving you a 'realistic job preview' of how your future day-to-day life could pan out. Running a business is very different to simply delivering your product – someone will need to be making sales, taking and fulfilling orders, keeping financial records, doing marketing, etc., so it is good to test out your possible future life and decide whether it is for you or not.

 Before committing wholeheartedly to your venture, trial it on a small scale to see whether there is a demand for your product, and whether it looks like you will be able to deliver it.

---

7. Deciding what action you can afford to take

It's just like any other budget. You have to figure out, what are my expenses? How much money is coming in? What's my break-even number?

Steve Rosko, So Cal TTC

At this stage of our journey we've done our business trial and it has proved successful. Low-scale operations are up and running on a pilot basis – we have a metaphorical queue of 60 customers outside each Saturday to collect their bread from the home bakery. But how do you now take this to the next level and start working in your 'shop' full-time?

During our research, we asked entrepreneurs how they made the decision that they could afford to scale up their venture from a trial to a full-time occupation. For example, how did Kate and Richard make the leap from being employed full-time and baking bread on a Saturday to opening up shop premises and working 100 per cent within their business?

The answer to this question was surprisingly simple and is summed up by Steve Rosko's quote above. You can attempt to answer it for yourself through two formulas.

Formula one: Working out your required income

Ongoing personal expenses
+ ongoing business expenses = required income

Typically, entrepreneurs calculated their personal expenses in one of two ways:

1. Working out what percentage of their current salary they needed in order to survive (e.g. I know I can live off 80 per cent of my current income).

2. Scrutinizing their daily/weekly/monthly/yearly outgoings and calculating how much income they need to cover this.

Some people were prepared to scale back to the bare minimum, cutting all unnecessary costs in their lives in order to realize their dream. Others could not make many cut-backs. It all depends on your own personal circumstances. But whatever your target, you need to be *very realistic* about how much income you personally need.

Ongoing business expenses varied considerably from venture to venture. Clearly a bakery employing eleven staff with ongoing costs for the business premises and raw materials has considerably higher ongoing costs than someone who is running, for example, a corporate training consultancy where courses are run at clients' offices. You will need to assess the likely outgoings for your venture.

The material covered in Chapter 9 should help you to explore at least some of the costs you will incur.

You may also wish to consider how revising your business model could lower your ongoing business costs. For example, if you want to go into the retail business, can you open an online store rather than physical premises?

Formula two: Working out how much capital you need

Start-up costs + financial buffer = lump sum requirement

In addition to funding ongoing personal and business costs, entrepreneurs also often needed an up-front lump sum, either to buy equipment or because they knew that they would earn a low proportion of their former salary during their first few months. A financial buffer was also required to buy them time against unforeseen problems or to finance unforeseen personal or business costs.

The size of your lump sum requirement will vary depending on your personal circumstances and the nature of your business, and you need to think through these demands very carefully prior to passing the point of no return.

Interestingly, many of our entrepreneurs did *not* seek lump sum funding from banks to give them start-up capital. The emphasis was on taking the venture live with minimum financial risk, for example, through using a loan from a family member that the family member could afford to lose. Other people knew that they could afford to earn no income for x months, because they could rely on the buffer of a family member or their personal savings. They took the view that if they couldn't get their venture off the ground, they would seek another employed role to get their income coming in again. There was potentially a risk to their résumé from doing this, which they also needed to factor into their decision-making.

 If other people are impacted by your income, such as a partner, or if you will be relying on them for a while, be sure that they are involved in this decision-making stage.

Don't bet the farm on your business, put enough in to have enough skin in the game, an amount that is meaningful but leaves an amount small enough for you to survive.

Stelios Haji-Ioannou, founder of easyJet

A real-life example of moving from a 'trial' to full-time commitment

Back in Chapter 4 we met Steve Roe, who started a comedy improvisation business called Hoopla. We described how Steve moved from splitting his time between working for Hoopla and contracting in television production companies to becoming employed on a full-time basis by his own venture. But how did he make the decision that it was time to leave the safety net of being employed?

Steve began by working out the absolute bare minimum that he could afford to live off. While working as a television runner, and earning no money from Hoopla, Steve could (uncomfortably) survive if he lived with his parents and removed all luxuries from his lifestyle. So this salary became his absolute bare minimum self-employment earning target.

Steve then began to test the market by offering free evening improvisation classes in a local pub, where he could use a function room without charge. After a time, Steve then decided to charge £1 per person for the class. Believe it or not, some regulars dropped out. However, others stayed and more soon joined, meaning Steve began earning money from his venture, albeit a *very* small amount.

As Steve began to generate income from an evening of self-employed work, he'd multiply his profits by five (for the days of the week) and then would multiply it by 52 (for each week of the year). This enabled him to constantly assess whether scaling up his business activity could generate his minimum income target. This led Steve to understand which products/services would be viable for his full-time business:

- Producing improvisation shows was costly in terms of time and expenses, and created low profit margins.

- Running drop-in classes for the general public had low associated expenses, but did not provide enough income to live off alone.

Increasing the cost of his drop-in sessions, running more of them, plus supplementing his income from these with classes in the corporate sector *did* make the business viable enough to become a single source of income and Steve was able to exceed his minimum earning target and move well beyond that.

- What are the minimum start-up costs of your venture? How can you finance these with an acceptable level of risk?

- What is the minimum amount of income – net of tax – that you can afford to generate in forthcoming months/years (including any buffer of savings that you have)?

- How can you finance your venture, achieving both sufficient time to make progress and also to sustain the costs of living?

- Think about the financial and other costs associated with your venture (e.g. distraction from your family/'day job'). Is there a point at which you will need to pull the plug or change direction if things aren't working out? If so, where is that point?

I worked out that I could live if we made what we made before, minus 10 per cent and I think that's what anyone should do. Figure out what is the minimum you can live off and see if that is acceptable. If you make $100,000 per year already and think you can't make a penny less, it is going to be very difficult if not impossible for you. Expect to miss paychecks.

Ryan Prettyman, Radiation Detection Services Inc.

 Tips for success

Once you've calculated what action you can afford to take, here are some tips from our entrepreneurs that will help you to swim (not sink):

- Aim to limit expenses to income wherever possible to ensure that you are not getting yourself into debt that you can avoid.

- Appreciate that business can be seasonal, so don't be tempted to splash out during times of 'feast', when you are better off saving for times of 'famine'.

- Take the view that you will be paying yourself last out of any income you make.

- Make sure that you have a buffer to get you through tough times. It can take many months before you can start earning a profit.

- Minimize your business costs – cut back to the bare minimum.

How could you apply the above tips? You may find it helpful to find other entrepreneurs to discuss their viewpoints and seek their opinion.

While you may have a viable business ready to go, you need to make sure that you can afford to give it the time and money in the start-up phase so that it has a chance to grow. Otherwise it will fail before it can be a success.

8. Making sure the price is right

Have the right product at the right price.
Sarah Hodgson, The Button Company

Determining what price to set for your products and services can be agonizing for any entrepreneur to get right. Even if you've been working in an industry for a number of years and are familiar with what prices there are for different offerings, are these the prices you could, or should, be charging?

If you set your prices too low you may never make enough income to make the venture work, and it can make people wrongly assume that your offering isn't *that* good. Yet, if you set them too high, you'll scare potential customers away. This chapter therefore concentrates on helping entrepreneurs to identify the 'right' price for your offering.

Approach A: Work out how much you need to charge

One approach to pricing is to work out how much it costs you to produce something and then add your profit margin on top. The formula for a cost-based approach to pricing looks like this:

Out of pocket expenses + Labour costs
+ Mark-up = Price

Let's explore how this formula works by imagining that we are selling cups of coffee in a cafe.

- Out-of-pocket expenses include consumables associated with the purchase (e.g. the coffee beans, serviettes and sugar) and ongoing business costs, such as rent, electricity and accountancy fees.

- Labour costs – the cost of your time or the time of others.

- Mark-up – the amount of profit you want to make from each sale.

There are limitations to this pricing formula. For instance, it is possible to deliver your services with no out-of-pocket expenses, without charging for your time, and with no mark-up. In other words the price can = $0, but does that mean that your product/service has no value to the customer who wants it?

There's a great piece of footage online that shows a violinist busking in a busy subway station in Washington DC. Let's imagine that the busker had walked to the station, he wasn't charging for his time and he wasn't aiming to make a profit – that's essentially why he can afford to stand and play for free.

However, it transpires that the busker was Joshua Bell, one of the world's leading musicians. He played one of the most intricate pieces ever written with a violin worth millions of dollars. Two days before his playing in the subway, Joshua sold out at a theatre in Boston and the seats averaged $100 each – that gives an indication of what his true market value is. In other words, the value of a product or service can be significantly different from the cost that you can provide it for.

Approach B: Work out your value

An alternative pricing formula could look like this:

Quality of product + Quality of experience + Scarcity + Benefit to customer = Value

Let's breakdown each element of the formula in turn to explore how it works.

Quality of product

Let's return to the coffee analogy. Put quite simply, what would you be willing to pay more for:

- A coffee made from instant granules that have been sitting round for a little too long?

- A coffee brewed from the finest quality, freshly produced coffee beans?

Assuming you like drinking coffee, you'll almost certainly have been prepared to pay more for the second option, so clearly the quality of the product contributes to its market value.

It's still worth remembering that some people will always choose price over quality, driven by their level of disposable income and their personal values, so even though they can see the additional value they won't want to pay the extra for it.

Quality of experience

Now let's take coffee beans from the same harvest. The quality of the product is now identical, and the beans go to two different destinations:

- A grotty café in a grim area of London, which serves coffee in plastic cups.
- An elegant coffee house, overlooking the River Thames and the Houses of Parliament, serving beverages in finest china, with a piano playing in the background.

How much would you be willing to pay for a coffee made from the same beans at each of these venues? You can see from this example that it isn't only the quality of what you purchase which drives its value, but also the experience that accompanies it.

Scarcity

Now imagine two scenarios, using yet more beans from the identical harvest:

- Scenario 1: The coffee is available from every single café across London.

- Scenario 2: There's only one café in the whole of London where you can get the coffee and there's a humongous queue of people waiting to buy it.

How much would you be prepared to pay to get your coffee in each scenario? Your answer reflects the impact that scarcity has on value.

Benefit to customer

Finally, let's imagine that you are on a first date with the partner of your dreams – the benefit of the date going well could be life-changing for you. Would you rather take your date to:

- The grotty café in the grim area of London?

- The one overlooking the Houses or Parliament?

You can see from this final example that where the stakes are high, you may be prepared to pay a much higher price. Why? Because although it is expensive there is a large possible return on investment, far more than the cost of the purchase, which increases its value.

People ask us why our prices aren't cheaper. It's because our guy is so specialist. He's very experienced and his skills aren't something you can easily get.

Ryan Prettyman, Radiation Detection Services Inc.

Your value may surprise you

Now let's focus on a real-life example of where an entrepreneur could potentially have undercharged for his services if he had failed to appreciate his value.

Andrew Gittins, Proposal Automation (launched 2010)

Andrew loved his job working as an account manager for a technology company that provided automated proposal software; technology that helps organizations to produce sales documents more efficiently. Then, out of the blue, his company merged with a major competitor and he was made redundant.

Andrew's role had involved selling one specific software product, which he had learned to use inside out. However, while working with clients he had also spotted an opportunity to perform contract work, marrying his own proposal-management experience with his skills in configuring the technology to get it working at its best. His hunch for the demand for this niche was confirmed when, shortly after his redundancy, he was offered a six-month contract, working in a finance company that had just purchased the technology.

Andrew faced a problem though. He had *no idea* how much his service was worth, particularly since he could not find anyone else in the world occupying this niche.

He could have taken Approach A to naming his price:

- Calculating his out-of-pocket expenses – Andrew would incur some business overheads, but there were relatively few costs as he was providing a service.

- Charging for his time – for example, looking at how much he was paid per day in his previous role to understand how much his time would cost.

- Adding in a mark-up – to cover downtime between contracts, or non-chargeable time such as invoicing.

However, rather than taking this approach, Andrew decided to seek guidance about his market value from the recruitment consultant who was placing him in the contract role. The result was that he calculated his daily rate based on the value-based approach.

As Andrew told us, 'I couldn't quite believe the numbers I was able to charge. I never thought I would be able to charge that amount of money for what I wanted to do.'

Taking Approach A to pricing would mean that Andrew's services failed to take into account how much benefit he could bring to his customers. Even if he charged a rate equivalent to twice his previous daily salary, this could still lead to a significant return on investment for the organization contracting him, which stood to make a lot more money from using their technology to its optimum. It also would have failed to take into account the scarcity of Andrew's services – remember that there was no one else in the world occupying that niche.

Andrew was awarded the contract role and his subsequent work received major recognition within the organization, with the project winning an award for being one of the best projects across the whole global firm. Andrew's achievement also became well known within the industry, with the software supplier that had made Andrew redundant using the project as a case study of how well their system worked at their user conference and as a reference to support their own sales!

Word of mouth about Andrew's skills then began to spread across the industry, and his services became in demand from other organizations as a result. His test of the market (through the contract role) and the resulting publicity enabled him to leave traditional employment behind, creating a strong foundation for his own entrepreneurial venture in which he also knew his value. The value of Andrew's work was evident in his self-employed pay-packet: he saw a 50 per cent rise in his first month's earnings compared to his best ever month as a sales rep.

---

1. Draw up a list of direct competitors for what you offer and study their marketing material and prices. If there are no direct competitors, you can study comparable products/services used by your target client base.

2. Reflect on:

   (a) How the quality of your product/service compares to others.

   (b) How the experience of your product/service compares to others.

   (c) How common your offering is.

   (d) How much benefit your product/service gives the customer in the long term.

3. Use the value-based pricing formula in Approach B (above) to have a go at working out your value.

4. Now use the cost-based pricing formula in Approach A (above) to have a go at working out your cost.

Overall you are looking for the 'value' of your products/services (output of step 3) to match or exceed the 'cost' (output of step 4). If you cannot deliver the value in the customers' eyes at a viable price, then you will need to rethink your niche and your offering.

Let the customer name the price

Here's a final tip if you are still struggling to set your price. One entrepreneur commented to us that when he didn't know how much to charge, he simply asked the client, 'What budget do you have?' The answer the client came back with was quadruple what he was intending to charge. Unsurprisingly, the entrepreneur was happy to match it!

When is 'free' the right price?

Our group of entrepreneurs had mixed feelings on the topic of providing anything for free, particularly because it can set a dangerous precedent that devalues your offering.

However, when you are in need of opportunities to showcase your venture, giving people a taste of what you offer can be a great way to build a network. Offering your products or services for free can make it a 'no-brainer' for people to do business with you. This helps you to understand whether there is a need for your product/service – if you can't even give it away, the chances are it will be very hard to sell it.

For example, you could consider offering your service on a voluntary basis for a high profile, worthy cause, where it is relevant to their enterprise. This will give you an opportunity to showcase just how good you are and could connect you to some great contacts. Plus, it enables you to get a client testimonial or case study under your belt, thereby increasing future clients' perception of your value.

Should you decide to offer anything for free, you may wish to consider placing a time and quantity limit on any free activity, and to think about which 'freebies' will really drive the outcome that you are looking to achieve. In other words, be selective about what you give away.

We donate birthday parties to local schools for silent auctions and they're a hit. It costs us to host the birthday but then we get 10–25 kids who've never been in this gym before, where it's fun, fun, fun and like Disneyland for two hours. Kids cry when they have to leave.

Steve Rosko, So Cal TTC

 The right price for your products or services is the price that your target market is willing to pay, and that is a result of the perception they have of the value of your offering.

---

9. Setting up the business infrastructure

The reason why we've built a company is because I think a company is by far the best way to get the best people together and align their incentives around doing something great.

Mark Zuckerberg, founder of Facebook

Once you've decided to take the plunge, the next step is to formalize your venture. This chapter will help you to work through how to set up a business infrastructure.

The formal business plan

Although the common advice to aspiring entrepreneurs is to write a formal business plan, we've been pretty surprised by how often this *doesn't* happen! We've seen many cases where people have gone on to run very profitable enterprises without one, so our research has found that you don't *have* to do this in order to succeed.

It is clear, though, that many successful entrepreneurs typically know what *would* have gone in the plan had they written it. They are aware of:

- The **core purpose** of their enterprise and what it is they are going to do.

- The **business's aims**, including specific, realistic goals or financial milestones that they want to achieve.

- Their personal **values** and how they want to go about doing business.

- What **products** or **services** they will offer to begin with, including an understanding of their unique selling points, niche, or hook they have to entice customers to do business with them.

- The **market** that they will be operating in (often derived from experience previously working in it) including an understanding of the competition and the market value of their products/services.

- Who their **customers** are, what they want/need and how you can meet their requirements (often derived from being within the market, or from testing the market by speaking to potential customers).

- Basic **costing** for the business and a subsequent **pricing strategy**, including an understanding of how they will fund their personal life and their entrepreneurial venture.

- Strategies for future **expansion** – the longer-term plan to grow.

- Logistical considerations, for example the **location** of their venture and the **assets** required for start-up, including a list of **suppliers** where applicable.

As you launch officially, you should aim to have a good grasp of the answers to these questions. Through reading this book and through your work to date on your venture, these answers should be becoming clear in your head. However, it can be good to pause and make sure you are confident in your answers.

TRY IT NOW! Using a couple of pages of paper at the most, begin writing down your 'business plan lite'. Use the bolded words we have listed in the bullet points above as headings and begin the process of committing to paper the fundamental basis of your venture.

The most valuable part of writing a formal business plan, to us, has been the process of planning. It's been a cathartic experience.

Peter Thomond, SportInspired

USEFUL TIP If you want to write a formal business plan, there are many free templates available online. Should you require funding, or a loan from a bank to help you begin your venture, more often than not you will need a formal business plan in place. Do check with the provider whether they have their own template that you are required to complete.

Legal status

When formalizing their business ventures, our entrepreneurs have had to consider the legal structure for their business, for example whether they offer their services on a self-employed basis, or through a limited or incorporated company. Each of these legal entities creates different implications, including what taxes to pay, ownership, liability of the enterprise, or the reporting they are required to do by law.

Our case study entrepreneurs have had to carefully consider which option is best for them. We've met some entrepreneurs who have chosen to trade on a self-employed basis, because it's a relatively straightforward option to set up, with lower ongoing cost and commitment compared to other options. For example, key legal requirements have included registering as self-employed with their government and completing self-employed tax assessments.

Other entrepreneurs have chosen to set up as a limited or incorporated company, which is a good option if you plan to employ anybody, or work with large businesses. This may even be a contractual requirement for some organizations to do business with you at all. Advocates of this arrangement have argued that although setting up a limited company adds to accountancy costs, and has created other statutory and financial obligations (i.e. having to produce annual reports), it also limits the loss that they could incur, should their business get into financial difficulty.

Legal requirements will vary from country to country and therefore we have not covered them in detail in this book. You should research the options for structuring your venture in your own locality and we recommend getting professional advice on this matter, for example from a lawyer or the person who is going to quickly become your new best friend – your accountant.

Your new best friend

The very first person hired by many of the entrepreneurs we spoke to was a professional accountant. Why? Because when starting an enterprise there's already a world of new responsibilities to get acquainted with, quite aside from having to work out how to do book-keeping and submitting annual accounts and the other filings you may need to do. An accountant can take care of this side of the business for you and leave you free to get on with making your business a success and growing it.

It's important to meet and interview your accountant before you commit to giving them your business. Like any relationship that's worth anything, it has to be built on trust and understanding. You each need to know where the other is coming from and your accountant needs to understand what it is your business seeks to do, in order for them to advise you properly.

- Draw up a list of people in your close, personal and professional network who may have an accountant already, either for their personal taxes or for their business accounts.

- Approach a number of your contacts, letting them know why you're looking for an accountant and ask them whether they can recommend one. A personal recommendation from someone within your network is invaluable when finding an accountant because somebody else has already tried and tested their services out.

Some important items to consider when setting up

Provided below is an indicative list of things to consider when setting up the infrastructure of your enterprise:

- **Registering a company**: if setting up as a limited company you'll need to be registered in the country you're operating from. There are restrictions on what your business can be called and it cannot be similar to a company name already on the register.

- **Notifying the government**: you may need to inform relevant government departments about your enterprise, for instance with regards to corporation or sales tax.

- **Regulatory bodies**: if your business is within certain professional service areas, such as psychology or finance, then you need to be authorized or regulated by a body to carry out work. In professions where there is no mandatory requirement it may be that there are voluntary bodies you are expected to sign up to and abide by.

- **Insurance coverage**: depending on your needs, you may require professional indemnity, employer's liability or public liability insurance.

- **Local authorities**: you may need to pay taxes for operating an enterprise from a premises, or have them inspect places of work for environmental or health and safety certification in order to attain the required permits.

- **Trademarks**: in order to protect your intellectual property you may want to seek registration of your trademarks with national authorities.

- **Business bank account**: unless you're self-employed, you'll need this in order to keep money earned and paid out from the business separate from your own personal finances.

- **Payroll services**: where you pay yourself/others a wage or a dividend, you'll need a payroll system in place. This is usually something your accountant can arrange for you.

- **Website domain name**: before committing to a trading or limited company name, it's important to check whether that name is available as a website domain. Even if you aren't planning to set up a website, it's cheap and easy to register the domain. It also prevents another business from taking that domain and receiving clients who were searching online for your business.

- **Licensing**: in some cases you may need to apply for a license, such as when you play live music or sell alcohol.

This list may look pretty long already but it's by no means exhaustive. Items are regularly added to the list of requirements for business owners. Consult professional bodies and industry contacts to ensure you maintain what is needed.

 Take a look at the bulleted list that we have provided above. Write down what actions you will need to take in each of these areas.

You may have noticed that, up until now, we have not discussed how to choose the name of your venture, a crucially important element of the set-up phase. If you'd like some inspiration and guidance, read on to the next chapter on branding your venture.

IF YOU REMEMBER ONE THING At an early stage it's important to get in place the infrastructure that will enable you to make your business a success, critically: your business plan, the legal structure of your venture and who your accountant will be.

10. Branding your venture

To be seen as a professional you have to create a brand that shows who you are and what you believe in, and that needs to be visual. A brand creates empathy and trust with clients.

Dianna Bonner, World Vision Photos

When a child is born into this world, we ask two key questions – is it a boy or a girl, and what's its name? The same is true for a business – what is it (i.e. what does it do?) and what is it called?

Just like your own name, you will use your business name every day, in emails, conversations or formally (i.e. when invoicing or quoting for business). Therefore it is a big part of your business identity. Naming your venture is one of the most important, as well as one of the most exciting decisions of your entrepreneurial journey.

This chapter looks at how to name your venture, as well as identifying some core elements of your brand that you'll need to consider to get your venture up and running with credibility and professionalism.

How do people choose their venture's name?

Using your own name

One of the most common ways of naming a venture is to use the founder's name. If the business is anchored around your skillset, then the business *is you*, so it makes sense that its name reflects your identity. Entrepreneurs often comment that success in business is underpinned by building personal relationships, and therefore using your own name makes your business personal.

However, entrepreneurs who have used their name also frequently advise *against* this. It makes the business harder to sell in future, should that be something you want to consider, as someone else may not want to take on your name. It can also make your business appear small, which could reduce your credibility in the eyes of larger clients. Plus, there is the issue that you may have other people delivering your business's product or service under your name; if you've made a bad choice in your employees, partners or associates, then they can damage your reputation.

That said, if you do choose to use your own name it doesn't mean that you must always be part of the business – just look at the success of McDonald's. The restaurant was founded in San Bernardino, California by the McDonald brothers and it was later purchased by their business partner, Ray Kroc. As you know, it is still one of the world's most famous brands.

> *I wanted to have my name as part of my business because clients know me by name and I have a certain level of credibility. It makes my business closely associated with me as an individual.*
>
> Jon Cuff, Cuff Jones

It does what it says on the tin

The better your name communicates to consumers what your business is, the less effort you need to put in to explaining it. Let's make up a fictitious name – 'Earth to Mars Shuttle Services'. From the name you could hazard a pretty good guess at what service the business provides!

When using the 'does what it says on the tin' approach you need to get the pitch just right – too broad and people won't know what you do. For example, what does a business called just 'Earth to Mars' do? On the other hand, if your name is too narrow, then it limits you. What would happen if you one day wanted to provide shuttle services to Venus as well?

A catchy, made-up word

Some business names aren't even real words. Take the name 'Google' for example. This is derived from the mathematical term 'googol', which means 10^{100} and reflects the huge quantity of information online that could be searched.

Using a made-up word is advantageous, in that it is less likely to be trademarked or used by someone else – something that you should definitely check when choosing a name as it means you could be met with a legal challenge later on and forced to change the name. A made-up word for a business name also shows that your business is different, which might be a quality that you want to convey as part of your brand. However, make sure that your made-up word is catchy enough to stick in people's memories and simple enough to spell. Just like learning a foreign language, it can be hard to remember new words, and you don't want to miss out on business because people can't remember what your business is called!

Remember that less is more

Think of some of the world's most famous brands: Nike, Apple, Coca-Cola, Toyota, Amazon and Vodafone. You will probably notice that they are all short and sweet.

People who have long names find it a pain to keep writing them, so bear in mind the practicalities of having a long-winded website or e-mail address. You can always shorten it to a nickname, but this can dilute your brand. Also consider the practicalities of writing multi-word business names when it comes to your website. Will it be easier for your customers to key in 'Earth-to-Mars-Shuttle-Services. com' or 'EarthtoMarsShuttleServices.com'?

- Brainstorm a list of potential names for your business. Enjoy the process and take your time, consulting with friends and family over your choice. Your business name is a really critical part of your business so the time considering what to call it is time well spent.

- When finalizing a choice, be sure to check that no one else is using the same name or has trademarked it. Also make sure a suitable website domain is available for you to register, as without this you may confuse clients or potentially lose business to a competitor who has that website already. To check the availability of a website domain, type the words 'domain check' into a search engine and you will be given a number of options for this type of service.

The brand behind the name

Once you've chosen your name, you can begin to develop the rest of your venture's brand.

Interestingly, some successful entrepreneurs believe that branding is irrelevant at the start of your journey, arguing that your business will be judged by delivery and results. Others argue that branding sells as much as the product and it is essential to get it right.

We believe that at a minimum it is essential that you look professional enough that people take you seriously.

The basics of your brand

When you go to the supermarket, there are some basic essentials that you always need, like bread, eggs and milk. Here are the fundamentals that you may wish to consider when it comes to your brand:

- A **font** to use as standard – serif fonts like Times New Roman may be considered more professional while sans serif fonts like Arial are more practical as they are easier to read digitally.

- A **brand colour** – consider the impact on emotions and connotations that different colours have and make sure you choose one that represents what you want to convey in your brand.

- A **professional logo** – your logo reflects your business so it needs to represent everything you want to convey in just that single image.

- A **letterhead template** – this is what you will use first and foremost for business correspondence. It should carry details about your business, including its contact details and address, legal structure (in the event that it is a limited company or partnership) and any applicable mandatory or voluntary registration numbers (i.e. for sales tax, or for your regulator).

- A **presentation template** – whether you'll be conducting presentations or just sending information to clients, you may have need for a PowerPoint template.

- An **invoice template** – when you've provided your product or service to clients you will need to bill them, so you'll require a template like your letterhead that itemizes charges and taxes incurred.

- A **proposal template** – when you're asked to provide a proposal for a piece of work you'll need a proposal template where you can detail what services would be provided, by whom, what experience they have and what the charges would be.

- A **website** – whether you plan to make the website into a store front for your products or just a place for clients to get your contact details, it should carry your logo and reflect your branding decisions. You'll find more information on this in Chapter 12.

- A suitable **email address** – if you want to be seen as professional then you will have an email address connected to your website, rather than a personal e-mail.

- A **basic description** of what you do – you need to convey 1) who you and your business are, 2) what it does and 3) for whom. You can then use this on your website, verbally with potential customers, or in business proposals.

- Relevant **networking tools** – business cards are a good way of providing your contact details face-to-face while online profiles on sites such as LinkedIn, Facebook and Twitter are great for virtual networking (we will cover social media in Chapter 18).

 The world is full of inspiration for your business brand:

- Jump online and study the world's leading brands. Look at their websites, fonts, logos and how they describe themselves.

- Look at the documents you've received from other businesses recently, such as invoices for your car insurance or letters you've been sent. Get a feel for the branding choices they've used and see if it provides you with inspiration.

- You can also find lots of templates on the internet or in Word and PowerPoint, to give you further ideas.

- Then have a go at constructing the basics of your business brand. Show helpful/supportive friends and family and ask them for constructive feedback. If you get stuck you can use specialist books or outsource the job. For example, there are professional service websites such as Upwork.com where graphic design specialists will compete to provide you with a logo at a price that you choose. Obviously you may get what you pay for, but it might give you some inspiration. It is worth noting that these websites have a multitude of other specialists who can help you with a wide range of business tasks.

Behaviour is also a brand basic

When people buy your brand, they are also buying your organization's behaviour, such as your ability to deliver on time, to keep promises and act with integrity. The next chapter therefore looks at your personal brand in more detail.

The brand you choose for your business will help define it to your clients within the marketplace, so it's important to make sure it represents and enhances what your business stands for.

11. Branding yourself

*I am a brand. And therefore I've got to look after my brand,
being careful what I say and what I do. Be everything that
you'd expect from a top brand – dress like it, act like it.
Think of your brand as something people will buy.*

Tricia Topping, TTA Group

Brands are all around us: they are well-known retail stores, cars on the roads, and products on our supermarket shelves. When we think of a brand, it brings up connotations about the quality of an organization, the pros and cons of using it and the experience that you will have when interacting with it.

Let's take McDonald's as an example. What expectations do you have about the quality of your meal? What are the benefits and drawbacks of eating at the place of the 'golden arches'? What experience do you expect to have when you are there?

Brands convey both reputation and expectations. They are based on our direct past experience, indirect experience (i.e. what you've heard from others) and represent our beliefs about future interactions. Critically, brands can apply as much to people as they do to products.

*Your brand is what people say about you
when you are not in the room.*

Jeff Bezos, founder of Amazon

REMEMBER THIS!!! Your personal brand represents your personal reputation created to date, and embodies the future expectations that people have of you. It leads to people making assumptions about how you will behave/perform in future and influences their decision of whether to do business with you.

Let's explore how to define your personal brand, and how to develop it to create the best possible reputation.

What is your current personal brand?

One of the entrepreneurs featured in this book described how he asked ten professional colleagues who knew him well to each give him ten words that described his personal brand. We thought this was an interesting exercise, so Alison decided to give it a go, using ten of our own business's clients. The results were really interesting. Because she was only asking for ten words, it clearly didn't inconvenience her business colleagues too much and she had a 100 per cent response rate to requests for feedback. So what did we learn?

- The feedback fell into three key categories: personal reputation, which is linked to the **products areas** that we work in (e.g. books/business/motivation); **skills** (e.g. 'organized'); and **personal attributes** (e.g. 'enthusiastic').

- While there were key themes, everyone had their own take, bringing unique perspectives to the party. Some words even contradicted each other, for example 'warm' and 'reserved'. This shows that although you are always the same person inside, you show different behaviour in different situations and this leads to different perceptions of your reputation.

- A few words represented behaviour that Alison had made a conscious effort to display. For example, since starting our own business she has made a very conscious decision not to get sucked into office politics, so she was pleased to see words such as 'professional' and 'diplomatic' on the list. However, even well-intentioned behaviour can have its downside, as this same behaviour was also described as 'guarded' by clients who said they'd like to see her let her hair down a little!

- Other words were the product of less intentional behaviour, which we wouldn't have used to describe Alison (i.e. 'intense'). On further exploration of the feedback, she found out that this was a flipside of some of the more positive terms that she had received, ones that she would be pleased to hear again: 'hard-working', 'diligent', 'focused' etc. But it is good to raise awareness of the downsides of your strengths, and consider whether you'd like to tweak your behaviour as a result.

- Many of the descriptors were heavily aligned with Alison's personal values – for example 'honest', which let her know that she is representing her business the way she wants to.

- Pick ten people who know your professional work well and who you think would be willing to help you explore your professional reputation.

- Simply ask them for a list of ten words that they associate with you and your work.

- Sort your list of 100 words into themes and explore the results. If there are any words that surprise you, go back and ask for further information.

- Finally, make a list of your personal values and see how much these align with your reputation. You'll probably be pleased if there is a good alignment. If there isn't you may wish to consider what has led people to misunderstand you and try to address the root of the problem.

Our business is an extension of our personal identities.
We built the company on our personal beliefs,
which represent the core of what we would and
wouldn't do. Never go against your values.
Deon Girdhar, Zay D Entertainment

What would I like my brand to stand for?

Once you know what your brand currently stands for, you can think about how to highlight its strengths, overcome weaknesses or build upon areas that it doesn't currently represent, but which you'd like it to. At this point you are making a conscious decision to develop the brand you have from just being you to having a potentially enhanced business identity, which is a conscious extension of your natural persona.

People buy people, and if they buy you, and they don't get what they think they're going to get, they won't stick around.

Cémanthe Harris, New Media Angels

We're not suggesting that you should undergo a major personality transformation – it would be hard to carry that off with integrity. Plus if you appear one way one day and completely differently the next, people can see you as inconsistent. However, we are suggesting that it is helpful to think about which aspects of yourself you'd like to tone up and tone down, in order to present yourself, and therefore your venture, in the best possible light.

There are three key ways we've found from our entrepreneurs when it comes to developing your personal brand. These are: 'looking the part', 'acting the part' and 'believing the part'. We'll give you some questions to help you think through how to develop each of these elements.

When thinking about these questions, consider how much of your personality you want to project within your business (e.g. your love for outrageous handbags), compared to how much is it helpful to tone down these elements to separate your personal identity from your professional one. Note that the answer to this dilemma will differ between entrepreneurs and industries, but it is worth making a conscious decision about how much of 'you' you want to deliberately project. Remember that your reputation will be influenced by a number of factors including how you portray yourself on social media sites such as Facebook – it isn't just how you are in person that counts.

Looking the part

- How do role models within your industry sector present themselves, in terms of their physical appearance?

- When you project your best possible visual image, how do you appear?

- How do you currently let yourself down through the visual image you project?

- What steps could you take to enhance your overall visual image, while remaining true to yourself?

Acting the part

- How do role models within your industry sector present themselves, in terms of their behaviour? What specifically do you see them do?

- When you are at your very best, what behaviour do you display?

- What behaviour have you previously displayed that has dented your personal reputation?

- What steps could you take to enhance your overall reputation, through being more conscious about the behaviour you display?

Believing the part

It's very difficult to act the part (e.g. being confident) if you don't actually feel that way deep down. So to change your behaviour, sometimes you have to change your underlying beliefs about yourself.

- What beliefs about myself help me on a day-to-day basis (e.g. 'I know my stuff')?

- What beliefs about myself hinder me on a day-to-day basis (e.g. 'I'm operating outside of my comfort zone'; 'I am not as competent as others')?

- What action can I take to change negative beliefs to ones that support me?

Look at the work output of industry peers and benchmark your standards against theirs. If your standards meet or exceed theirs, your confidence should grow. If your standards don't stack up so well, consider how you can look to improve your output, so over time you gain more confidence in yourself.

If you want to learn more about the impact of beliefs upon success, and explore in more detail how to change them, take a look at our sister book in this series *A Practical Guide to the Psychology of Success*.

 Your reputation and people's expectations create a brand around you. It's worth identifying what that brand is, seeing if it's what you would want to portray, and enhancing those areas that you want to accentuate more than others.

12. Setting up your website

Because of the internet, business has moved from being about 'what can I do and who wants it' to being 'what are people looking for and how can I provide that'.

Steve Roe, Hoopla

A website is where your venture comes to life in front of a global audience. It reflects your brand, showcases your products or services and acts as a shop window for new clients. There is a wide variation in levels of sophistication of websites, influenced by the needs and expectations of your target market, the practicalities, such as your (or your friends') website designing skills, and your budget. Wherever you decide to position your website, from basic to flash, one thing that entrepreneurs in our research agree on is that your customers will expect at least a basic website, so this chapter explores the practicalities and considerations when setting one up.

Planning your website

A website is like a building – you may want to rush in and start constructing it so that you can immediately benefit from it, but it's going to stand stronger if you have a plan in place first that you adhere to. When it comes to websites, knowing *why* your target market will want to visit it, *what* it will contain and *how* it will look enables you to make sure that you build it to be fit for purpose.

Why will your target market want to visit it?

There are two key groups who will be visiting your website: potential clients and existing clients. The needs of both groups will be different so it is necessary to consider their needs separately.

Potential clients might visit your website for a range of reasons, for example, to see who you are, where you're based, what your venture does, how much products or services cost, to buy something they've seen elsewhere or to find out how to contact you for an enquiry.

By comparison, existing customers will know the answer to some or many of those questions already. When they visit your website they may be looking for updates on your venture's activities, newly released products or services, what else you offer, how to contact you about an existing order or to place a new one.

 Put yourself in the shoes of an ideal potential customer. Why do you think that person will visit your website? Write down a list of ten reasons.

Now imagine that potential customer has become an actual customer. Why do you think that person will now want to visit your website? Write down a list of ten reasons.

What it will contain?

Once you've considered why visitors will come to your website and what they're looking for, you'll need to satisfy their needs by ensuring the website has the right content. Through visiting the websites of a number of enterprises we found the following common themes that you could consider including:

- **Purpose**: This taps into why the venture offers what it does, to whom, and why this is important.

- **People**: Details of who the people behind the venture are, so that visitors can review experience and credentials.

- **Products/services**: Like an online brochure, a website can detail what it is the venture does and for whom, so that visitors can see if it is something that they want. In addition to describing what a venture does this could also feature videos or examples demonstrating exactly what is provided to clients.

- **Contact details**: A quick and easy way for visitors to see how to phone or email, including where offices/shops are based (if relevant for clients to visit).

- **Store**: This is so visitors can add products offered by the venture into a shopping cart, that they are then able to order and, where applicable, have delivered.

- **Advice**: People search the internet looking for answers to specific questions, so a website containing relevant information could attract them to visit (i.e. posting links to new research in a field related to your venture). This often takes the form of a blog.

- **Social media**: Links to a venture's Facebook, Twitter and LinkedIn profiles make it easy for visitors to then connect with your venture and its people online. Websites often contain sections on a page showing the latest status updates or tweets the venture has made.

- **Achievements**: To build credibility this can include details of awards that have been won, lists of clients and client testimonials about the products and services they received.

- **Newsletter sign-ups**: Visitors who are interested to hear what your venture has to say can provide their e-mails and get periodic updates.

Take a look at the websites of competitors or other suppliers within your industry. What content do they have on their website that also serves the needs of potential clients and existing ones?

How should it look?

Once you know what it is that you should be including on your website you need to consider how it will appear to visitors. As the online presence of your venture it should reflect the brand identity that you've identified in Chapter 10. This includes combining elements such as font type, colours and the logo so that visitors will know that they've arrived at the site for your venture and not somebody else's.

Also important to consider is the layout of the website, for instance, how will visitors be able to navigate around your site? Will your website have artwork and images, or will it be text-based?

 When using images that aren't your own you'll also need to consider issues like permissions and quality. For instance, if you need an image from a stock photo library you may have to pay for a license to use it to avoid copyright issues. Images you use online can be at a low quality (referred to as 75 dpi); however, should you want to print the same image in a brochure you would need a higher quality image (300 dpi).

 Go back to the websites of competitors and other suppliers that you looked at before and identify how their layouts differ. Which provides the easiest layout to navigate that you could use as inspiration for how your own could look? You may wish to produce a rough drawing of the main pages of your website on paper or in a program such as PowerPoint.

 We recently met someone from Google who explained that their organization has an internal mantra, 'Mobile comes first'. With the rise of smartphones, people are increasingly searching online through their mobile phone. Therefore, when building your website you should ensure that the layout is compatible and that its speed works well if you are accessing it through a smartphone.

Building your website

Once you have the plan for what your website will include and what it will look like, you will then need to consider how to go about constructing it.

Domain and hosting

The domain is what somebody types into a browser to find your website, for instance 'CNN.com' would take you to CNN's website. There are a number of online companies who will allow you to search what domains are available so that you can register the one that you want. Note that visitors often expect a website to end '.com' if it's a company, unless it is targeted at a certain geography, for instance '.co.uk' for the United Kingdom.

Companies that allow you to register a domain will also offer a hosting service, which is an online storage facility that allows your website to be up and running 24/7 and is therefore essential. You'll want to look for hosts that provide facilities to create email addresses for your domain name, a suitable storage size for what you'll have online (i.e. photos, downloadable brochures etc.) and adequate bandwidth, which determines how many visitors your website can receive.

Designing the site

Once you have the logistics set up you'll need to configure the layout of your website and add content. The most basic option is often to use the free templates that the hosting services provide, which give an easy and quick way to set it up, while allowing you to customize some parts to fit with your own brand (i.e. the photos shown, the website colours, etc.).

For a more intermediate approach, consider using programs like WordPress or Joomla, which are content-management systems (CMS) that easily allow you to change the layout and text on your website but enable you far greater customization. A good host will have instructions on how to set up a CMS, usually with only a few clicks of a button. Because these systems are so popular there are many guides online that will walk you through the process of building your website.

Few of the entrepreneurs that we spoke to went with the most advanced option, which is learning how to build a website from scratch using programming languages like HTML. Instead, for more complex sites they tended to have an expert website designer produce their website for them. There are plenty of companies out there who would be able to help you get your website up and running. One place to consider looking is on Upwork.com where you can detail what it is you need and then relevant providers will offer you competitive prices to perform the work for you.

 If you don't build your own website make sure that it is designed in a format that you can easily edit. The content of your website is likely to evolve over time, so make sure that you have the ability to update it yourself, to reflect your changing needs.

 A website is your online presence that allows you to tap into a global audience of potential and existing customers. By building a website with the needs of your target market in mind you'll create a useful, centralized place for information about you, your business and the services you offer, as well as a place for customers to purchase them.

13. Get the assets and equipment to launch

We started up in our living room, setting up some tables with our computers. When we started employing people we moved to the garage. When that became too crowded, we bit the bullet and rented our first real office.

Susan Heavilin, MicroTest, Inc.

Many ventures are trialled and launched using only minimal equipment, such as a laptop, printer, phone, car and the kitchen table. Often these resources are owned already, which has the major advantage of avoiding up-front expenses before you've made a penny in return.

For other ventures, it would be impossible to start up without a major investment in physical assets. However, some entrepreneurs use their budgets more wisely than others. This chapter therefore looks at how to use your precious cash wisely, and avoid debt as much as you can.

Steve Rosko, So Cal TTC gymnastics facility (launched 2008)

Clearly to run a professional Trampoline, Tumbling and Cheerleading (TTC) club you need more than a laptop! So how did Steve Rosko start a club that, within five years of opening, has become one of the top five largest trampoline teams in the United States?

Steve and his five siblings had grown up in a gymnastics club. They were there so often with their mum that she got offered a job working there! His mum was then asked to manage the club, and eventually she owned it, and employed her teenage children as coaches. Steve therefore knew *everything* there was to know about the industry.

As an adult, Steve continued to work in the industry and over time came to be employed by a local TTC club. However, after five years of working there the club hit financial difficulty, so the then club owner decided not to renew the lease on the gymnasium premises. He approached Steve with the opportunity to take over the business.

And here's one of the secrets behind Steve's success: he knew when to say no. The business was failing, and the price that the owner was offering was simply too high for him to afford, what with a wife in full-time education and a young baby to support. So, although he was on the verge of signing the paperwork, Steve made the decision that the venture simply was not viable and walked away.

Three months passed and then the owner approached him again, offering the lease for a second time, but now at a *third* of the price. Admittedly, the package did not come with all of the expensive equipment that it previously would have done, but critically, it came with all of the basic equipment that he needed to get started. This time the deal *was* right and Steve took the chance to start his own business.

In the early days the club simply used trampolines that were a quarter of the price – totally safe to use and good enough for the students at that time. But Steve's club is now proud to coach four children who are on the United States national team. The club therefore needed to own trampolines of a quality used in international competitions. Over the years, Steve has been able to sell his original equipment and replace it with far higher quality materials, including the international-grade trampolines. Importantly though, at the outset, he knew what was good enough to get his business going and didn't take on more expense than he needed to.

Equipment isn't the only asset in your business – location of the premises is also critical. Steve's facility is located in an affluent area in California, with an estate of million-dollar homes just around the corner. Steve believes that in times of recession (which did subsequently hit) kids' extra-curricular activities can be among the first expenses to go. However, being located in an affluent area has buffered Steve from this problem. He says if he was to open another club, then location would be one of the first things he'd consider.

He also comments that, when you lease your business premises, the relationship that you have with your landlord is critical. Steve is blessed with an excellent working relationship with his landlord, who has the philosophy that Steve's success is his success. Steve's landlord has therefore been very supportive when Steve has made reasonable requests to him.

Although it may not be something that you think of as a problem when starting out, when money is tight, several entrepreneurs in our research have commented that they wish their business premises had more space. Steve has worked hard to use every square inch of the premises, so that he can increase the number of simultaneous classes from a maximum of two, to seven. But he still doesn't have all the room he would like. Remember that if you have plans to grow your venture, you need to consider what space you will grow into.

The final stroke of genius behind Steve's success is his funding arrangements. When the gym was originally at risk of closing, several parents of club members really wanted the facility to stay open, as their kids loved it. They strongly believed in Steve's credentials as a coach to their kids and knew if anybody could make a TTC club succeed it would be him. So they offered him a very favourable loan with a flexible repayment schedule. Five years on from purchasing the business, Steve's club has grown to 500 members and he has now paid back virtually every penny. It just goes to show that you don't need to be at the mercy of banks to get much-needed funding.

THINK ABOUT IT

- What is the bare minimum of physical equipment that you need to get started?

- What is the right physical location for your venture? How much space will you need to grow into?

- How will you fund your start-up costs? Remember that there are more options than bank loans. We've found that loans/financial support from family members are particularly helpful to aspiring entrepreneurs when they are carefully thought through, communicated and agreed.

- How can you cut costs? For example, through using second-hand equipment, or negotiating lower rents?

- How can you protect your assets? For example, if you invest money improving a premises to make it fit for purpose, how can you then ensure that you aren't kicked out by your landlord and lose your investment?

Choosing your suppliers

Unless your product or service is skills-based it's likely that you will need to be able to source supplies in order for your business to sell anything. Your choice of suppliers may be limited to one exclusive provider, where you have no choice but to go to them, or you may be able to choose from a range of different suppliers, in which case you need to determine the best ones for you.

Don't just look at the price of your suppliers, look at the service they provide too. We had ordered a huge mixer that was too heavy for us to move. The supplier just left it on a pallet on the pavement and wouldn't bring it inside for us.

Richard Copsey, Holtwhites Bakery

Our entrepreneurs have told us that local, smaller suppliers have proven to be better for them as they have more passion for what they're doing and will go that extra mile for you. Keep in mind though that as your business grows you will be looking for your suppliers to be able to grow with you, without compromising the quality of their service.

- Draw up a list of the supplies you will need to get your business started.

- Identify people in your network who are in the same industry as you. Contact these people and ask them whom they can recommend for the supplies you've listed.

- Alternatively, ask people who provide a similar service to you but who you aren't directly competing with where they recommend you get supplies. Our entrepreneurs have told us that these people are usually more than happy to help, as it's their way of sharing the passion for their business.

Suppliers may not always see the bigger picture and may fail to appreciate that the longer your business is trading for, the better it is for them. Some might be in it just to sell the supplies they have and not see beyond that. Remember to only buy in exactly what it is that you need by identifying it in advance of any negotiation.

To get your business going you may need to increase the assets and equipment you have, in which case, make sure you limit your purchasing expenses as much as possible and buy only what you need from suppliers you trust.

14. Communicating that you are open for business

Get people in the door, any which way you can.
People have got to find out about you.

Steve Rosko, So Cal TTC

You can have the best products or services available, but they are worthless if no one knows that you exist. Therefore when you are ready to launch you need to put time and effort into spreading the word. Here's how one entrepreneur did it.

Beverley Christie, Beauty Sensation (launched 2007)

Beverley offers beauty services at her clients' houses and also has a purpose-built treatment room at her own home. We know from personal experience the high-quality services she offers, including massages, manicures and facials.

Prior to 2007, Beverley had been employed in the beauty industry for a number of years and greatly enjoyed her role. However, she was fed up with low salon wages. When she was made redundant, Beverley decided to launch a mobile beauty business, because they were popular in other areas, and at that time, there was only one other mobile beauty therapist in the area. Beverley therefore decided to accept the risks associated with a temporary drop in income, and made the sacrifice of selling her car to purchase a van, which would enable her to transport her equipment from client to client.

One of the most inspiring aspects of Beverley's story is the dedication and simplicity of how she got started. Having first tried advertising in a local newspaper with lacklustre success, she pounded the pavements of her local area for four to five hours every day for six weeks, posting several thousand price lists through letterboxes. Beverley took her diary and mobile phone with her as bookings would come in while she was still out delivering! Some of her clients from that initial leaflet drop are still her customers today.

Since the leaflet drop, word of mouth has been Beverley's killer weapon, because she's reliable, flexible, offers a range of products and is able to cross-sell across her range. Remember that if you are good at what you do, it is priced correctly, and there is a demand for your product/service, people will recommend you and will keep coming back. But critically, potential customers have to know that you are there in the first place. The leaflet drop was Beverley's magic key to raising enough awareness to get her business started.

If, like Beverley, your first attempt at marketing doesn't work well enough, don't give up. You've probably already done the hard work to get your business ready for launch, just try something different and eventually things will click into place.

Why did leaflets work for Beverley?

Beverley's leaflets worked because of three key reasons: 'WHO', 'WHAT' and 'WHY'. You need to consider each of these aspects carefully when communicating about your venture:

- ***WHO: Know who you want to target.*** Beverley wanted to target customers in her local area and decided that leaflets were a cost-effective way to spread the word to them. She picked her letterboxes carefully, for example targeting roads that were close to a salon that had recently closed.

- ***WHAT: Make it very obvious what you are offering.*** Beverley used price lists which succinctly covered all of the basics that people needed to know about her business, including the services that she offered (with an indication of quality by featuring branded treatments), transparent pricing and contact details. If her leaflet came through your door, within seconds you'd know *exactly* what she was offering.

- ***WHY: Know why you add value.*** Beverley's proposition was to offer a better beauty service than the local competition. She aimed to offer a good range of branded treatments, in the comfort of clients' own homes, at very competitive prices (made possible by her low overheads). Note that she's picking up on the key niche factors from Chapter 5 – quality, service, price and location.

Try our four-sentence challenge to see if you can communicate the WHO, WHAT and WHY of your venture succinctly.

Complete the following sentences:

- I work with _____ (WHO: name your key customer group)

- They have a need/desire to _____ (WHY they want your product/services)

- My venture offers _____ (WHAT your core products/services are)

- So that they _____ (WHY clients benefit from using you)

This exercise may seem simple but if your venture is quite complex (i.e. you have multiple products and multiple target markets) your sentences end up being anything but succinct. Remember that if you can't describe what you do, then it is going to be very difficult for your customers to understand how you can help them.

Having a complex business can lead to a temptation to repeat this exercise multiple times for multiple products/client groups which then leads to a variety of different marketing strategies. However, be warned that this can make life very complicated. For example, entrepreneurs comment that, when selling multiple products to diverse markets, they need different ringtones on their phone to alert them to which type of call is coming in. Your venture can also appear to lack credibility to clients if you seem to offer everything under the sun.

We're not saying don't have a wide product range – if you've got a client pool with diverse needs, it can be good to have options for cross-selling. However, you need to have an overarching core purpose, which can be easily communicated and act as an umbrella for everything you offer underneath that.

Other strategies for communicating that your venture exists

So far we've focused on using leaflets to communicate that you're open for business. While leaflets were very successful for Beverley they may not be for other services.

There are many ways you can communicate that your venture exists to potential clients. Here are ten strategies used by our entrepreneurs to market their ventures in the early days:

1. Advertising/free publicity in publications (local or specialist)

2. Paid/free publicity online, using marketing directories or social media

3. Setting up a website with search-engine-optimized keywords

4. Cold calling/emailing (i.e. contacting relevant people they've not been in touch with before)

5. Attending networking events and meeting useful contacts

6. Tapping into networks gained through previous jobs

7. Tapping into personal networks

8. Speaking at events, where they can raise their profile

9. Showcasing what it is they can do at trade shows

10. Volunteering to showcase their services and build new relationships

These are all marketing methods that have been used in real life to market ventures in the early days of business. Each of them enables an entrepreneur to communicate the 'WHO', 'WHAT' and 'WHY' to an audience. Some may be better than others and some will be more appropriate for your specific venture.

 Different methods work best for different ventures. Which methods do you think will work best for your venture?

It's all about making a connection

We've all groaned as we put the phone down on another annoying telesales call; however, sometimes they do work. For example, Ryan, who you will meet in the next chapter, recently received a cold call asking him if he wanted an 0800 (toll free) number and he answered, 'Yes!' He'd coincidentally been researching them as he'd been thinking about getting one. So he pointed out that telemarketing does work if you make a connection with people who want your product/services.

The same thing happened when we were looking to hire a cleaner. Having trawled the internet, not really knowing where to start, a leaflet from a local cleaner dropped through our door and we ended up hiring her services for several years. If you know your target audience, remember that they might be really pleased to hear from you and what it is you have to offer, as it will save them the time and effort spent looking around.

Other traps to avoid

Costly marketing strategies: There's been one very consistent message from the entrepreneurs we interviewed and that is: don't waste money on expensive advertising in your early days. Many entrepreneurs admit that they spent money advertising in newspapers and magazines and often the result was absolutely nothing! In addition, while you may think that glossy brochures will impress new clientele, be aware that your core business could evolve considerably from its early form, rapidly making early marketing literature obsolete. If you do choose to invest in glossy brochures, the advice is to avoid doing this up front.

Negative self-fulfilling prophecies: When marketing your venture in its early days you also need to be aware of your personal beliefs and make sure they don't become self-fulfilling prophecies. For example, if you keep telling yourself that cold-calling/emailing large organizations will never work and you never try as a result, that's a sure-fire way to guarantee you will be right! Although psychologically it may feel much easier to place an advert in a publication than to pick up the phone, remember how much cheaper and more personal a phone call is. If you've done the groundwork you'll now have a good product and understand who wants it and why, so when you pick up the phone have the confidence to tell people how it will benefit them. You never know who's looking for precisely what you have to offer.

You'll find out just how useful dreaded cold-calling can be in the next chapter, which concentrates on converting leads to sales.

IF YOU REMEMBER ONE THING Once your venture has launched you need to communicate to your target audience what it does and why they'll benefit from it, so that you can build awareness and start bringing in customers.

---

15. Converting leads to sales

When potential clients know who you are, and they know where you are, they will come to you when they're ready.

Cémanthe Harris, New Media Angels

In the previous chapter we said that the best product/service is worthless if no one knows about it. However, it's also worthless if everyone knows about it and no one then uses it! Therefore this chapter concentrates on the topic of how to convert leads to sales.

Ryan Prettyman, Radiation Detection Services Inc. (RDSI) (launched 2010)

Ryan and his business partner Matthew Doering spotted a potential gap in the market to specialize in the sale, service and installation of radiation detection systems. Within a couple of years of launching they have made sales across most US states and internationally, as far afield as China, India and Peru. So how did they convert a good opportunity into an enviable sales record in such a short period of time?

In the early days, Ryan did a lot of cold-calling. He got a list of 1,000 names and looked at it, thinking, 'This is going to be horrible but at least by the time I get halfway down, I'll be pretty good at it.' And did he get good at it!

Ryan's advice regarding cold-calling is to not come across

as a sales person, but to use the opportunity to get to know the person at the other end. 'Most people hate telemarketers, and you rarely make a sale at the first attempt anyway, so you need to break through the barrier and convert a 'cold call' into a 'warm call', whereby people already know you when you speak to them. Contact people, build relationships and concentrate on giving them information that is genuinely helpful. The more you talk to them, the more likely they will be to call you with a sale down the line.'

Once your foot is through the door, your next challenge is to convert a lead to a sale. Ryan advocates a killer weapon for this: persistence! For example, Ryan knew that RDSI could provide a great service to a particular Fortune 500 company. However, at that time, there was a ratio of three RDSI employees to a company with 400 nationwide sites, making it a case of David and Goliath. Impressively, over 90 emails and 100 phone calls later, which helped to build a relationship, RDSI was rewarded with a one-off trial contract.

Your second killer weapon is preparation. When you've done the hard work to get in the door you need to ensure that you don't mess up. When Ryan first met with the Fortune 500 organization to try to win the trial contract, he prepared for the meeting as if it were a job interview for his dream role. He knew everything about the potential client and had anticipated their questions. For example, when the Fortune 500 company challenged Ryan about the 'David and Goliath' issue, he responded by asking the meeting attendees if anyone played golf. When a golf player identified himself Ryan then asked, 'Would you rather play with someone who has ten years of experience and is pretty good, or a young Tiger Woods? That's what we are, we are that good.' Ryan had carefully thought through all their possible objections and could answer them with well-thought-out strategies.

Ryan's story shows that a bit of *pain* (from having to do cold/warm calling), plus *persistence* and *preparation* pay off when aiming to generate leads that convert to sale.

Obviously you then need to deliver on your promises and realize the benefit of all of your hard work. In the example of RDSI, the trial with the Fortune 500 company went well and earned them another ten trials. This ultimately led to an enviable nationwide contract, which has given RDSI a great foundation for future success.

Other tips when closing a sale

We've talked about the importance of the three Ps (Pain, Persistence and Preparation) when aiming to convert leads to sales, so what other factors support successful sales? Here's some advice from our entrepreneurs:

Listen to a customer's needs and tell them how you can meet them

Although you may have a target demographic, within that, customers will have their own needs. The more you understand exactly what the customer wants, the better placed you are to decide whether you can tailor your product or not, and communicate how you will meet their precise needs. If you can offer the same product as a competitor in a way that better meets the needs of a customer then it may be the difference between making or losing a sale.

Be clear about what you will deliver

At the point that you are closing the sale it is very important to specify (possibly in writing depending on the nature of your business), precisely what you will deliver, by when, and include any requirements that you need from the customer in order to fulfil the delivery. Making sales involves managing expectations, otherwise you can go to the effort of delivering for the customer only to find that they won't pay you, or they demand a refund/re-working because their expectations were not met. This can be very costly to you in terms of time and money and can potentially damage your reputation.

Don't over-promise but do over-deliver

While it can be tempting to market yourself in the best possible light, it is also important not to promise things that you cannot hope to fulfil. Although you will lose out on some sales because of this, it means that when you do make sales, you are likely to be able to deliver in a way that meets the client's expectations. Making a sale isn't only about closing the deal, it's about fulfilling an order that the client is satisfied with.

Avoid pressure-selling tactics

Although these are used successfully by some organizations and they can work, particularly where it is a one-off sale that counts, they can also lead to customers feeling bamboozled into a purchase and regretting doing business with you. If you want to build a long-term relationship with a client, or you want them to refer you to others, avoid a hard sell. Instead, focus on keeping in contact with people enough to remind them that you are there. Give them everything they need to know about you, help them wherever practical and accept that clients will approach you when they are ready. If you've got a good product/service, at the right price, and you've raised enough awareness about it to the right target audience, then it should sell itself.

- When have you been on the receiving end of an outstandingly good sales experience? What were the factors that made it so excellent? How can you apply this to your own venture?

- When have you had a terrible sales experience? What were the factors that made it so bad? How can you avoid replicating this when making sales yourself?

You are aiming to find a win-win outcome

Remember that it is your job to find the win-win situation that makes the sale. What makes the 'purchase' work for both parties so that it is a 'no brainer' to do business?

Although you may be desperate to make sales to bring in revenue, don't forget that the deal has to work for you too. You have to be confident that you can deliver what is being requested, within acceptable timescales and at an acceptable cost. In other words, you are aiming to find a way to provide value to your clients that is both realistic and achievable.

 While you may need to step outside of your comfort zone to generate sales, by demonstrating persistence and preparation, and seeking win-win outcomes with your clients, you'll convert those who have a need for your products or services into customers.

---

16. One lead leads to another

Treat your clients as if they are friends. Try to help them. Be loyal to them and they will reciprocate that. Customers who aren't current customers still refer clients to me.

Cémanthe Harris, New Media Angels

Entrepreneurs can feel overwhelmed by the need to generate new leads in order to break into new target markets; you just cannot see a way through what seems like a brick wall. So we want to inspire you that simply *taking action* can generate the leads you're looking for. Taking action opens new doors, ones that you never knew existed and can ultimately take you to very exciting places.

Dianna Bonner, World Vision Photos (launched 1999)

Dianna had a love and passion for photography from an early age. Even as an eleven-year-old she could be found carrying her camera, getting into all different kinds of odd positions to try to take that perfect scenic shot.

At the end of the 1990s Dianna was working in a very different profession, travelling around the world on the tennis circuit supporting the young female players. However, she realized that she had the potential to earn a living through photography when her employer stopped hiring a professional and asked her to take their group photographs instead. Her images were so good that they were published in the national media and were regularly used in marketing material for her employer.

When Dianna's job was put at risk due to an organizational restructure, rather than reapplying for a role she didn't really want, Dianna decided to follow her passion and become a professional photographer. Fortunately, she already had invaluable entrepreneurial experience through her early career running two businesses abroad, where she had gained expertise in sales and marketing. This supported her decision to take the plunge.

And here's the key: when you adopt the attitude 'I'll just give this a go', it's amazing what doors open to you:

- Dianna's first step was to arrange a sales meeting with the *Photographer's Handbook*, to try and decide whether she should advertise in it. As luck would have it, the sales lady (who loved Dianna's work) happened to know someone who needed a photographer for a hen night and Dianna found her first client without even advertising for it!

- On the evening of the hen night, Dianna struck up conversation with one of the 'hens' who happened to be organizing a summer party at work and asked Dianna to attend and take photographs.

- At the summer party, Dianna made contact with other professionals working on the event. She subsequently worked in partnership with them for three years, taking photographs at events they'd organized.

- While photographing events Dianna met yet more clients. She was careful to pick up listings of event attendees, so that she could research and contact possible new clients to make them aware of her services.

In other words, when Dianna opened one door she found another door to open, then another, and so on.

Dianna's approach to meeting new contacts through events, plus other forms of marketing (including networking, social media and e-mail), has led to her attaining an extensive contacts database. Dianna now has far more business than she can carry out herself and therefore has a team of photographers working for her across the UK.

And if you'd like to know where a passion for photography can lead, as well as owning her own studio and working on behalf of blue-chip clients, Dianna has photographed a range of well-known people at some prestigious events. These have included the entrepreneur Richard Branson, celebrity chef Jamie Oliver, and the British Prime Minister, David Cameron. That's not a bad outcome from something that used to be just a hobby! Plus, critically for Dianna, her business has enabled her to tap into the reason why she was so passionate about photography in the first place. She believes that a single camera shot can influence and make an impact that in some way makes a positive social and environmental change – an area she hopes to develop more and more in the future.

If you give your client a good service and value for money they will happily recommend you within their own network.

Beverley Christie, Beauty Sensation

 It only takes one lucky break to meet a contact that will open great doors for you. If you take action, you'll be amazed at what opportunities will come your way – things that you couldn't have planned, but which have a habit of appearing when you have an eye out for them.

What are the ingredients that lead to referral opportunities?

Yes, a little bit of luck does get you a long way (although it's funny how you can make your own luck). But luck isn't everything. There are several other key factors that really make a difference when generating leads from leads.

1. Be good at what you do

Imagine if Dianna had sat down with the sales representative from the *Photographer's Handbook* and had shown her a whole range of photos that were distinctly amateur. How far do you think she would have got? In order to be recommended you need to have a base level of competence. Be realistic as to how good you are, and understand when it's time to leave a hobby you love as just a hobby.

2. Be reliable
Now let's imagine that Dianna had messed up with her first client, for example she'd got the date wrong and hadn't turned up at the hen party. If you mess up, you miss your opportunity to impress, and damage your reputation in the process. One of the most important factors for entrepreneurs is to *do what you say you will do*. If you're naturally disorganized then you'll have to plan around this (e.g. getting someone to help you) because you can't afford to be unreliable.

3. Be pleasant to interact with
It's human nature to judge whether or not we like people and whether we've enjoyed an experience we've just had. Sometimes even if there's a great product on offer, the thought of interacting with an organization or individual can be enough to turn you away. Interestingly when you stop and think about your own 'bad experiences' with organizations, it isn't often the product that makes you mad, but rather a rude, thoughtless or uncaring attitude that accompanies it. Looking at the other side of the coin, building a great relationship with prospective clients can be one of your greatest sales tools.

4. Be responsive

Building on the previous point, it's also extremely annoying as a customer when you are trying to communicate with an organization but you can't get an answer. When we were trying to organize a cleaner and requested a number of quotes we couldn't believe the lack of response that we got! They instantly lost our business. If someone can't even return your call, it doesn't bode well for whatever service they would offer you in the future. Being responsive does potentially impact on your work–life balance. It means that you may be on holiday when a client request comes in and you have to suspend your tanning and deal with the request. But your reputation is on the line and unfortunately this can be part and parcel of running a business. We'll talk more about how to cope with this in Chapter 22.

5. Be honest and fair

If you can't deliver it's best to be honest up front rather than letting somebody find out later. It's better to under-promise and over-deliver. Where there's been a mistake be quick to listen to the customer's point of view and demonstrate a 'bounce-back recovery'. In other words, if you've dropped the ball on their expectations, go out of your way to make up for your mistake and impress the customer. Sometimes your recovery can be a great opportunity to show just how good you are and how much you care, and can lead to great loyalty and recommendation.

There's nothing more powerful than your customer
going to people you'd love to work with and
saying 'You ought to work with these guys.'
Peter Thomond, SportInspired

Getting the ball rolling

While referrals are a great way to gain new business, clients may not always be immediately forthcoming in providing them. They may be too preoccupied with their own life to consider what is important to you.

If you feel like your product or service has performed well for them it doesn't hurt to ask the question at the time, or soon afterwards, 'Is there anybody else you know of who could benefit from my product/service?' This can be a great way of getting the referral ball rolling.

Of course, a client may not always know of an immediate opportunity that they can refer you for. In this case, you could ask them if they would be happy to provide a written testimonial for you. You can then use this on your website or in other marketing materials, which gives an indication to a potential client what your previous customers appreciated about your products and services.

Organizations face risks when taking on a new provider,
so you want to take a good testimonial or referral in
with you. Just ask your existing clients for them.
Andy Carley, Response Development Training

- Approach five to ten people who have been customers in the past or who you are currently working with.

- Ask them to provide a testimonial about you and the product you provided or service you delivered.

- Reflect on the question, 'How can I use existing clients to generate new referral opportunities?'

Referrals are a great way to grow your venture. Simply by taking action and delivering on what you offer, you'll be able to open doors to opportunities you otherwise wouldn't have known existed.

17. Networking

You're never going to win business by sitting in your house. You've got to go to every event in your sector. Do anything that puts you in touch with people.

Tricia Topping, TTA Group

When you are in the early stages of developing an entrepreneurial venture it is clearly desirable (and a challenge) to raise your profile. This often tempts entrepreneurs to try different networking avenues, from attending formal local networking events to spreading the word to friends and family, or popping out for coffee with industry contacts.

The results of never-ending networking can certainly be frustrating for entrepreneurs. Attending networking events for local businesses can merely result in carrying home a pile of irrelevant business cards, and having one-to-one lunches with industry colleagues can be pleasant, but often no opportunity results.

You can see how failed attempts at networking can equip entrepreneurs with three basic beliefs: 'I hate networking', 'I'm useless at networking' and 'Networking doesn't work for me'. It is quite easy to understand why some entrepreneurs therefore avoid networking and give up using it as a marketing tool.

However, as well as the 'misses' there are 'hits' too. For example, Cémanthe Harris, a social media entrepreneur who you'll meet in the next chapter, analyzed all of the business that her venture generated during the first year of trading and concluded that 48 per cent of her business came from formal networking events. Remember that there are many different ways to network and your challenge is to find a tailored approach that will help you to make it a 'hit'. This chapter therefore looks at how to make networking work for you.

Adopt the mindset of 'How can I help you?'

Although intuitively you might go to a networking meeting with the mindset of 'How can you help me?', it's fascinating what happens when you take precisely the alternative view.

We were recently invited for coffee with a new industry contact called Mary (a friend of a client) who was hoping to break into a niche similar to ours. In truth, in years gone by, we may have politely turned down a request of this nature thinking, 'They can't help us; this is just going to be a waste of our time.' But we decided to try out a tip from one of the case studies in this book, which was to accept the next networking meeting that you are offered and to simply go with the attitude of 'How can I help you?'

What you don't necessarily appreciate when taking this approach is that when you help someone you are unconsciously showcasing your knowledge, passion and expertise at the same time in a very authentic way. And here's the interesting part of the story: less than four weeks after the coffee meeting, Mary heard of a piece of work that wasn't yet suitable for her but recommended us instead. Having genuinely expected nothing, we were rewarded with a valuable lead for a great piece of work.

It is sobering to reflect on how, in the past, we would have tried to 'sell' to our network with lacklustre success, and how much more effective the exact opposite approach turned out. Plus, meeting with Mary was so much more enjoyable than some of the other 'networking' approaches we've taken in the past, because it wasn't just a sales pitch. If you're in business to improve the quality of your life, remember how important it is to *enjoy the journey*.

> *Networking isn't, 'let's work together – do you want to buy from us?' It has to have mutual benefit, say information sharing or something like that. Then sales will come. The best way to establish networks is to provide value with zero expectations and then it will come.*
>
> Ryan Prettyman, Radiation Detection Services Inc.

Less is more vs. more is more

So how many networking opportunities should you make? This is an interesting debate in light of our meeting with Mary described above. If you're not careful you could spend all your time meeting people for coffee, leaving you buzzing with caffeine and doing very little actual work.

Our view is that there is a balance to be struck, which reflects how established you are. In the early days, if you have time on your hands, you may have little to lose and a lot to gain from trying diverse networking opportunities. Diversity allows you to test new strategies for raising your profile and you might find one networking avenue that really clicks. Plus, entrepreneurs comment that it can be comforting to have contact with other people who are in the same boat, for example through attending local networking events. It also forces you to get good at articulating what you do.

However, more experienced entrepreneurs advocate being far more selective when dedicating specific time to networking, giving the advice that, 'There's no point giving up your time at night and then going out and spending it with the wrong people.' This is especially true where you have a very niche product.

That said, successful entrepreneurs also are typically adamant that networking is at the heart of their business success. They've learnt that you have to get out, tell people about what you do and focus on raising awareness with the right people. Often the emphasis is not on selling but on building relationships and nurturing them, which later turns into sales or leads to other useful relationships.

Networking without deliberately networking

The above debate also relates heavily to your definition of what networking is. On the one hand you *can* do too much formal networking: if you spent every day for a year attending formal networking events, and didn't actually produce anything, you aren't going to have a successful year.

However, you can look at networking in a completely different light. Assume that it's impossible to meet too many people. Don't just confine networking to formal meetings but see it as any opportunity to meet people, whether at a dinner party or at a local community event.

With social media tools now woven into the fabric of everyday life, it's very easy to connect with someone, keep in contact and get to know them better over time. And those are the twin essences of networking: raising awareness that you exist and building relationships.

You can never do enough networking, it's impossible to meet too many people. Network everywhere, not just the places you think it's important to. You're networking all the time, not just when you're in a professional environment, you do it down the pub, on the plane, anywhere and everywhere.

Richard Stephenson, The Westminster Challenge

Tips for networking success

Here are our entrepreneurs' top ten tips for successful networking:

1. Wait to be asked the question about what you do before you tell somebody. Watch people's eyes as you respond to gauge their interest in you.

2. Recognize the signs when someone wants to leave or change the conversation about your venture – know when and how to end the dialogue.

3. You need to remember who you have met and they need to remember you. Online networking sites such as LinkedIn are very good ways of staying connected.

4. Relationships go cold over time, so devote energy to keeping them warm.

5. Don't approach networking with a view of trying to sell.

6. Ask your clients to introduce you to their contacts who may need similar services.

7. If you are attending an industry event, phone the organizers beforehand and get a copy of the attendee list, then research and identify the people that you want to meet.

8. More generally speaking, work out whom to target. Who would be a great person to know about your venture? Then try and work out a way to join the dots to that person.

9. Aim to create an association with the right people for your venture, then find a way to get in with them.

10. If the people you want to network with don't have a forum to meet, create one for them.

- Look back at the chapter and make a list of all of the different ways that you can network. How do these methods translate into your own world?

- What other ways can you build relationships with people and spread the word about your venture? Think about generic networking opportunities and then try and translate them into specific opportunities for your niche.

- Pick one networking strategy, opportunity or event that you think that you should try. Make a commitment today to do it.

IF YOU REMEMBER ONE THING There are many ways in which you could network, just remember that your core aims are to raise awareness of your venture and build relationships. Networking is at the heart of successful entrepreneurship, so if at first you don't succeed, keep going and eventually you will reap the rewards of it.

---

18. Using social media to grow your venture

Social media drives a lot of traffic. We have over 1,200 followers and the majority are customers. When I put a photo up of a new fabric, people come back to me asking when it's going to be put up online so that they can buy it.

Anna Hodgson, The Eternal Maker

If you're of the opinion, 'I don't get how social media can drive sales in my venture', you're not alone. However, many entrepreneurs now rave about it being the way of the future for business marketing, whether they are offering unique products, or their own skills and services. So let's start with a simple example of how social media (including Twitter, Facebook and LinkedIn) can be a great catalyst to an entrepreneurial venture.

Cémanthe Harris, New Media Angels (launched 2010)
New Media Angels specializes in helping businesses with their digital communications, with the main output being social media. It's always nice when organizations 'walk the talk' so it is interesting to see how social media helped Cémanthe to kick-start her own business venture.

In the previous chapter, we described how in her first

year of trading, Cémanthe met nearly 50 per cent of her clients at formal networking events. Another key marketing strategy that Cémanthe used was offering free seminars on how to use social media, for example in libraries or at events for small businesses.

Cémanthe's first sale followed a free seminar at a local library on how to use social media, where she simultaneously marketed her one-on-one paid coaching services. She successfully engaged a client from the seminar, who attended a one-on-one session, and followed Cémanthe on Twitter.

Cémanthe then came across an interesting report on social media, and she decided to 'tweet' about one of the statistics in it. Cémanthe's first paying client then 'retweeted' this statistic, which led to a new contact getting in touch with Cémanthe, who wanted to know about its source.

The new contact was someone who worked in a similar field, but was not a direct competitor. Cémanthe spoke on the phone with this person and they got on well and kept in touch. Then the contact started referring business to Cémanthe! This has been the source of multiple contracts for her, which now forms a very steady chunk of her venture's income.

THINK ABOUT IT

What interesting information related to your venture's industry have you read recently which you could share on social media?

Social media builds relationships

It's also interesting to explore how social media has played a role with our own relationship with Cémanthe, and the impact this can have on her business.

She met David through a drama group several years ago, before she had started her business, and we haven't seen her in person for over five years. Alison had only actually met her once in person before. However, when we met up with her to do the interview for this book, it was a bizarre feeling for Alison as she felt like she knew Cémanthe very personally. Many times over five years she's read her posts on Facebook so although she isn't Alison's 'friend' in the traditional sense, Alison knows what's going on in her life, who she works with and even what she ate last week! Cémanthe knows lots of random information about Alison too, plus they've commented on each other's posts now and then, so they have kept in touch.

So when we eventually did meet, it felt like we knew each other really quite well. This made it much easier to do business and also created a useful base level of trust and respect – which is probably why she was one of the first we invited to participate in the research and why she accepted our request without a second thought.

In turn, it's possible that readers of this book will be interested in her services, and that this could open doors to new clients for her. Now reflect on the power of social media: if Facebook didn't exist, the chances are Cémanthe would have dropped out of our lives and we'd never have known about New Media Angels. As a consequence, she would never have been in this book and you would be reading about somebody else entirely different right now.

 In the previous chapter we commented that networking is all about raising the awareness that you exist and keeping relationships warm. Social media is a very easy way to do this.

There is little distinction between word of mouth networking and social networking but there is a significant difference – social networking is much more engaging and personal.

Deon Girdhar, Zay D Entertainment

Laser-focused targeting

Although you might think of social media as a somewhat scattergun approach, whereby you put out information into the ether and wait for something to come back, Andrew Gittins (who we met in Chapter 8) is using LinkedIn in an ingenious way, which brings new leads right to him every day.

You may remember that Andrew's venture involves working with people who have recently purchased a specific piece of software, which Andrew then helps clients to use to its optimum potential. While this is a very convenient niche, Andrew faces two key challenges in his venture.

Firstly, people who use the software don't necessarily realize that they could benefit from Andrew's help. People often don't know that there is more advanced functionality that would solve problem points for their business. So they may not be looking for Andrew's services, even though they might benefit from them.

If clients aren't looking for him, this means that Andrew has to find them, which leads onto the second key issue. Andrew doesn't know which companies have recently purchased the system. So they don't know they need him, and he doesn't know who *they* are.

Therefore Andrew suggested to his old employer that they set up a LinkedIn group to share best practices about how to use the software. It's good publicity for the product and a great resource for its users. Andrew regularly contributes hints and tips to help members of the group.

But here's the really clever part: the LinkedIn group enables Andrew to see exactly who has purchased the software, as they will often sign up to the group. He can then connect to them through the group and begin building his relationships with them. Genius.

Social media gives access to free advice

While social media is a great source of free advice, remember that you can benefit from receiving as well as giving it. In fact, social media can give you instant access to experts across a whole range of topics. So have a think about what you want to know – there are many willing people out there who are happy to give you an answer.

For example, in Chapter 6 we introduced Richard and Kate who set up their own bakery. As well as using social media to interact with their customers they also use Twitter to put questions to other bakers. If they rang a baker to ask these same questions, Richard says that they would probably charge.

> *We have a Facebook group and other people write on it as much as we do. People post articles about bread, or mention how they enjoyed eating something nice from our bakery. It does generate clients for us.*
>
> Richard Copsey, Holtwhites Bakery

Your venture ... going viral

To help you to understand the power of online articles, here's an example of something that happened just last week. David has a love of writing screenplays and one of his goals is to get a script turned into a major film. David had been reading a number of books recently to help to improve his technique and learned about an online screenwriting magazine called 'Script'. He visited their website and saw that they had a Facebook group and 'liked' the group. This meant that whenever the magazine posted an article to Facebook, he would hear about it through his Facebook news feed and would be able to reap the rewards of some new hints and tips.

Sure enough, an article of interest by Hayley McKenzie popped up in David's Facebook news feed, and he was enjoying reading it, when he was surprised by some familiar words linked to the mindset of success for aspiring screenwriters. Quite by chance (we've never had any contact with the article author or the magazine at all) he spotted a quote from and a reference to our first book, *A Practical Guide to the Psychology of Success*!

We then linked to the article on our personal Facebook pages, thinking our friends and family would enjoy seeing the quote, and tweeted the link to the article on Twitter. Our link was then re-tweeted by our publisher, Icon Books and all of a sudden we'd publicized the article to thousands of people. (Plus you are reading about it now!) That just goes to show how one small reference online can lead to significant publicity.

 In order to get the most out of social media have a go at doing the following:

- Find people on Facebook, Twitter and/or LinkedIn that say or do things that are of interest to your target client group and share or link to the piece so that your network can benefit from it.

- Create a blog on your website and whenever you add an entry to it, share it via social media.

- Connect with your contacts and use it as another method of communication. For example, if a client has told you they have a specific hobby and you see something interesting about it, send it to them personally via social media and not email.

There's one last thing to say on social media and that is, 'It's not about self-promotion'. If you use social media solely to continually tell people about your product or service then they will quickly become disengaged. They will vote with their feet and 'unlike' or 'unfollow' you because you have nothing interesting to say. You wouldn't watch TV to just watch all the commercials and skip the content of your favourite programs would you? In the same way, nobody uses social media just to see your advertising. So keep the self-promotion communications to a minimum unless you do have something to shout about, such as an award you've received, or something to promote that will be of benefit to your customers, like a limited-time-only sale.

 Social media is a great way for your venture to reach an ever-expanding number of people. Done right, it can generate new relationships and new business opportunities.

---

19. Marketing your maturing enterprise

I was so moved when a client nominated me for Business Woman of the Year Award. When I shared the news on social media, people were so complimentary, I got lots of glowing comments from people I'd never met.

Cémanthe Harris, New Media Angels

So far this book has covered a number of marketing strategies, including setting up a website, communicating that you are open for business, networking and social media. While the strategies that we've mentioned are all great things to keep doing and build from, there are some other useful marketing activities that you may wish to consider, which are particularly helpful once your venture is a little more established.

Do I need to spend money to make money?

Now that you're up and running, you should have much more confidence and clarity over what your venture provides and who your core target market is. This might mean, perhaps for the first time, that you have profits that *could* be spent on focused marketing activities. So should you part with your hard-earned cash?

Interestingly, you've probably now learnt more about the value of money. If you were previously employed you may have pressed 'Print' on your work computer without too much thought. Now that you know that every page you reel off costs your venture money – money that you may have sweated blood and tears to create – you'll likely be more conscious as to whether or not to incur that expense.

Before you start spending significant money on new marketing activities, let's first consider what you can do for free, or with relatively little capital outlay. Here are eight different ideas for you:

1. Enter for an award

Awards are a great way to raise your venture's profile within your industry and also more widely. There are many awards out there for you once you start looking, from local enterprise awards to those for national excellence. Sometimes you'll need to submit a proposal as to why you should be considered; other times a third-party nomination might be enough for you to be shortlisted, which you can ask a client to submit for you. The award will raise your credibility and show that you are making waves in the industry.

2. Positive features in the press

Members of the press are regularly looking for experts who can provide insights on news stories. By making yourself available to them, explaining facts and providing valuable information, you may be able to feature in articles that they write or footage that they shoot. When you appear in newspapers, magazines or on TV it positions you as an expert in your industry and raises your profile at the same time. To help you to feel confident, and to ensure that you make a positive impression, you may wish to invest in some media training. This can be a wise use of your hard-earned cash if you intend to use this strategy effectively.

3. Speak at prestigious events

A number of our entrepreneurs started off speaking at low-key events. This gave them an audience who were very happy to listen, even as they developed their public-speaking skills. Now that their ventures are more mature and they have become accomplished speakers, they have been invited to more and more prestigious events. This may not lead to direct sales but it does continue to grow their network. Plus, speaking at a high-profile event is beneficial to your credibility and looks impressive on your website or social media newsfeed.

4. Create a bank of testimonials

As your client list grows and grows, so too does the potential number of testimonials you have available. By having testimonials from a range of people, you can be selective about the ones you use. For instance, if you were pitching for business with a school, having a testimonial from another school's headmaster is likely to carry more weight with a potential client than one from a director at a brewery.

5. Systematically keep in touch with clients

By collecting the contact details of your clients and any visitors to your website, you now have your own audience who are ready to hear what you have to say next. By collecting these into a Customer Relationship Management (CRM) system, such as Salesforce, it means that you can contact them with news or relevant updates. Perhaps you've launched a new product, given some valuable insight in a journal, or done something else of note that you want to share. Having your contacts in one place is an easy and simple way of notifying them of your latest news. Some CRM systems are available for free, although some entrepreneurs recommend paying for them, arguing that this is the best possible investment of a marketing budget.

6. Use sales reps working on a commission-only basis

Getting your products before potential customers doesn't mean that you have to pay for the privilege up front. Some of our entrepreneurs use commission-only sales reps to gain new clients. These people are out and about distributing a range of products, so if they can find customers for you they will then generate their commissions from selling your product. That makes it a win-win relationship for you and the sales rep. There may be suitable sales reps already within your network or contactable at trade shows.

7. Aim to replicate success

It's also important to remember that once you've found a strategy that works, you can simply aim to replicate it. For example, we saw how important cold calls were to Ryan from Chapter 15 and how this strategy led to his organization winning a major nationwide contract. Rather than become complacent and think, 'Phew, we're successful now, no need to do any more cold calling', Ryan is even more determined to make use of a marketing strategy that has a proven track record. So this year he's set himself a strategy that he's nicknamed '100:100:100'. He's going to send 100 emails to 'warm' leads, make 100 cold calls and send 100 cold emails.

8. Give away low-cost products as a thank you

Having giveaways for existing and new clients is a great way of delivering that little bit more benefit to them. Whether it comes to sending out t-shirts, your latest book, or even just a 'thank you for your business' card to clients, the personal touch can go a long way. It shows that you're thinking about them, that you value them and that you like them as a client. Just think how powerful that message is if you're on the receiving end; it's not often somebody that you've done business with expresses their appreciation in such a way.

We try to make every one of our clients partners. If we get a new client we send them a t-shirt. People do wear the t-shirts, it gets them involved. Everyone loves free stuff.

Ryan Prettyman, Radiation Detection Services Inc.

REMEMBER THIS!!! Even when you do have money to spend on marketing your maturing venture, remember that you don't have to splash out to keep raising your profile.

THINK ABOUT IT
- What other effective and relatively low-cost marketing strategies have you come across that haven't been covered in this book so far?

- How could you combine some of the above methods with others to magnify their impact?

Keeping track of your progress

When trialling new marketing strategies it is important to understand the value of your time and any financial investment you have made, big or small.

Many entrepreneurs are big fans of marketing metrics – tracking your marketing activities to see which convert into customer leads and which leads convert into sales. They highlight the importance of understanding how paying clients heard about you, so that you can replicate success and avoid wasting marketing budgets and time on ineffective strategies.

- Find records of any sales that you have made to date.

- For each client, work out how the client first heard about you and analyze what marketing methods you used to produce that sale.

- If you don't know, think about how you could find out, or how you could put strategies in place to find out in future.

Invest wisely in marketing spending

If you are confident that marketing spend is likely to pay off – perhaps because your competitors use that avenue regularly and you can see that it drives business for them – and you can afford it, then it could be worth a try. Several entrepreneurs do indeed advocate using more costly marketing activities because they know that they pay off for them.

For example, in Chapter 5 we introduced Anna Hodgson, who sells Japanese fabric and other craft materials. She has repeatedly marketed her products at trade shows because they drive sales during the event itself as well as creating valuable repeat business afterwards. Plus a trade show presence led to Anna's company supplying major high-end retail organizations.

Anna has also found that advertising in the right publications provides her business with a return on investment. She regularly places a big splash advert in highly relevant trade magazines, just prior to a trade show, as she knows that drives a queue of customers outside her booth. But she also has an eagle eye for marketing metrics. For example, she'll often include a 10 per cent discount when quoted in conjunction with the advertisement, so she can see exactly which clients have come to her through her advertising. This enables her to determine which publications don't produce a return on investment, in which cases, she stops advertising with them.

- Make a list of all the activities you could use to market your maturing venture.

- Ask yourself, for each strategy, how much time or money is it worth investing to make one sale?

 As your business grows you'll want to continue employing the marketing strategies that have worked so far, try out new ones, and be cautious about spending money on any activities that might not provide a return on investment. Metrics are a great way to see how investments of time and money in marketing activities pay off, and help you to understand whether to turn the marketing dial up or down.

---

20. Offering new products and reaching new markets

*If you go down the niche approach then you can take
on that next niche, then a next niche, then a next niche
until you take your venture to the mainstream.*

Peter Thomond, SportInspired

In this chapter we'll look at how to take your venture to the
next level by expanding your product/service range and
through reaching new target markets.

**Martin Stephenson, Hunts County Bats
(launched 1981)**

Martin's passion in life was cricket. So when
a good friend of his suggested there was an
opportunity to acquire the equipment and stock
of a local cricket bat factory that had gone into liquidation,
Martin was intrigued. He'd been a part of his father's floristry
and landscaping business for years and had learned the
ropes of being an entrepreneur. He therefore decided to
put in a ridiculously low offer for the liquidated company's
stock with his partner, just to see what happened. To their
surprise their offer was accepted!

While there was already an established customer base
for the stock that they had taken on, when those supplies
ran out they would need to be able to produce more. To

satisfy demand they decided to take on the services of two bat-makers and the factory manager from the liquidated company, renting new factory premises so that the team could make new stock. These three individuals were so efficient at production and sales that neither Martin nor his business partner needed to be involved day-to-day, which was useful for Martin, who was still working with his father.

With the cricket bat factory in full swing, Martin made the decision to wind down his involvement in the other business and concentrate on growing his own venture. History had already revealed that attempts to grow a cricket bat factory by expanding production and the size of the workforce hadn't worked. Therefore Martin and his partner decided that in order to take their business to the next level they needed to scale outwards, not upwards, expanding from being a cricket bat manufacturer to supplying other products within the cricketing world.

Martin and his partner spotted the opportunity to expand by diversifying from being simply a wholesale distributor to being a public retailer. This decision arose because they knew of a cricket retail business, which, like the original cricket bat factory, had over-committed and failed. Martin and his partner could apply their experience of hiring staff from the failed company and build a new retail business, providing them with a new channel through which to sell their range of products in the process. Having a retail outlet has also meant that they've been able to start supplying cricketing equipment to schools, which has tapped into a great new market.

Another excellent opportunity for diversification came when they set up a new wholesale company, one that acquired exclusive rights to sell prestigious brands of cricket helmets, pads and gloves. This meant that without manufacturing any new products, they could take advantage of cross-selling to their established sales networks.

Expanding in this way added diversity to their business interests and enabled Martin and his partner to develop a solid reputation within the cricketing supplies industry.

Martin is most proud of setting up where previous companies had failed, getting the best of the experience from staff that the failed companies had left behind, and making each venture thrive. Perhaps best of all, the three original staff that he took on from the old cricket bat factory still work at the new factory, and do a great job keeping it running and keeping the cricketing world supplied with top-quality bats.

- Would the purchase of an ailing venture be a good way to grow your own enterprise?

- How can you take advantage of cross-selling to your established client base? What else might your customers wish to buy from you?

- Is it appropriate to diversify your business to reach a new core target market?

Your sales channels and client relationships are a major asset of your growing venture. You've worked hard to get your foot in the door and establish your credibility. Now you should consider, how can your venture further benefit from this?

Investigate what else your clients buy

Martin knew that people who purchase cricket bats also need other equipment in order to play. He also recognized that if you supply top-quality bats, it's likely that your target market will value a wider range of similar-quality products.

It is important to realize that you don't have to actually *produce* more products in order to sell them. As you'll see in the next chapter, some businesses make money through selling other people's products through their existing sales channels. As long as the quality of sub-contractors meets or exceeds your established reputation then you could make more profits with relatively little work.

 How can you understand what other related products/services your clients use in order to identify opportunities for cross-selling?

Listen to what more your customers want

The best source of ideas for where your venture could go next may be from your most valued clients. As experienced buyers, they can spot trends across your industry and identify gaps that are ideal opportunities for you to develop into.

Some of the entrepreneurs we interviewed used this approach to great effect. They were approached for products or services that were outside their current scope, but they embraced the opportunity to expand their portfolio of offerings and delivered it. This not only led to a happy customer but also meant that they could add a new service alongside their existing core offering.

For example, Beverley Christie, the mobile beauty therapist from Chapter 14 constantly listens to what her customers are looking for, such as manicures using the latest UV technology to ensure that nail polish lasts longer. If Beverley believes there is enough demand, she will undertake additional training so that she is able to provide a wider range of services. This is a win-win situation. Beverley's customers can take advantage of having a convenient one-stop shop for a range of products, including ones that are hot off the press and in demand, and Beverley can offer multiple treatments to the same client, therefore increasing the amount of time she is delivering her services during her day.

Note that although Martin expanded his business by moving into new niches (e.g. wholesale to retail) Beverley didn't actually change her niche. She's still operating the same business model, but is offering a richer range of services in that niche. So it is possible to develop your business within your original niche, as well as beyond it.

Clients who request new products/services from you are like gold dust because not only are they telling you what you need to do next to succeed, but they are probably also identifying themselves as your first client for it. When clients are asked for their opinion and they give it, it's almost like they're becoming a partner in your business. Your success provides more benefits to them – if you have a more stable future from expanded offerings, and you can supply them with more of what they need, you're making their lives simpler all round.

When we first started we had a very basic service, but we really listened to the clients. They would say, 'If you could just do this too, then we can use you for both projects.'
Ryan Prettyman, Radiation Detection Services Inc.

 THINK ABOUT IT How can you get feedback from your customers on what they think of your current offerings, and what more they would like to see from your venture in the future?

Remember that each product or service expansion that you consider should be approached with the same principles and caution as your initial business idea. So as we've described earlier in this book, consider experimenting with any new offering in the most low-risk way that you can.

 Selecting a niche to start your venture doesn't mean that you are restricted to it. Once you can, and in the most risk-free way that you can, branch out your products and services that complement your existing offering and increase your value to your clients at the same time.

21. Growing your venture through win-win relationships

It's all about the relationship, it's not business-to-business, it's people-to-people. The relationship is king. Just being able to do what you do with that one new person, in any way you can, allows you to develop that relationship.

Andy Carley, Response Development Training

While it's true that ultimately you have responsibility for making your venture successful, you also have the opportunity to create a number of 'win-win' relationships with other parties, with the ethos 'you scratch my back, I'll scratch yours'. By partnering with these third parties, you have the opportunity to utilize each other's networks, relationships and knowledge for mutual benefit. This chapter therefore looks at how you can harness these opportunities.

Andy Carley, Response Development Training (launched 1995)

An outdoor education provider employed Andy for ten years, running outdoor training activities with groups of adults and young people. Then, one day, Andy was informed that the training centre where he worked was going to be sold.

Rather than simply accept redundancy, Andy and two colleagues decided to attempt a management buy-out.

They set about creating a business infrastructure to support their bid; however, their proposal did not win, coming second out of six.

Although Andy and his partners weren't able to purchase the physical business premises, their buy-out attempt had led them to create a business infrastructure that they *could* still use. Plus, over the previous ten years, they had developed positive relationships with former clients that money could not buy.

Andy and his partners therefore decided that they could pursue their business venture, but without the added burden of a physical building. They would simply make their product mobile. Their personal reputation for providing outdoor training was strong and before the end of the year they already had two former clients on their books.

After a few years, the three business partners realized that they each had different aspirations for the future, and it became clear to them that it needed to change. Andy therefore took sole ownership of the business.

It was at this point that Andy took advantage of a great opportunity to grow his business through collaboration. In an industry with a number of small businesses offering a multitude of services, some corporate clients were awash with choice. As a result, they preferred a one-stop shop for all of their training needs and so used the services of very large providers who would then organize whatever training was required.

The larger training providers then worked in partnership

with a number of smaller training providers who would actually deliver the services on their behalf.

Andy decided to tap into this 'win-win' relationship. The large company got the opportunity to market Andy's niche business (team-building and management development with an outdoor twist), expand their product range and take a cut of Andy's fees. In return, Andy received clients through this relationship without having to do the marketing.

This also meant that Andy had the opportunity to work with people that he otherwise wouldn't have, for example blue-chip organizations who prefer to work with other blue-chip suppliers. Andy was able to develop new relationships with clients at big-name companies, who then gained first-hand experience of Andy's business and its services. This meant that when they moved to another company and came to need Andy's niche training, they knew who to call.

I don't believe in competition I believe in collaboration, we can do things better together than apart. It is more important the client gets the service they need. I have referred clients to other providers and then, when they want further services, those clients come back to me.

Cémanthe Harris, New Media Angels

Collaborating for 'win-win'

As an entrepreneur it may be tempting to think that most other ventures are competitors and that if they win business, you lose it. This takes a 'win-lose' mindset. However, Andy's case study demonstrates that if you're prepared to collaborate rather than compete it can be a fantastic opportunity for both ventures.

Other businesses, especially those that are more established, may already have a large client base available to them but because of a limited product range, are missing out on opportunities to cross-sell. By making your offerings available alongside those of another venture, you provide a ready-made expanded proposition for them that is 'win-win'. Your joint-venture partner can demonstrate added value by making new products and services available to their clients, while you can gain access to a new, yet established, client base.

Remember that a joint-venture relationship can work both ways – you can also market other people's products and services to your own customer base.

> *Our success has really been based on partnerships from the very beginning.*
> Bill Gates, co-founder of Microsoft

- Draw up a list of key suppliers in the same industry as your venture that target the same client base as you do.

- Research what niches they cover and what products and services they offer.

- Identify if there are any gaps in their coverage of the market – it may be by location, product, service, quality, price, etc.

- If there is a gap in their offering where yours could fit, approach them with the suggestion that you collaborate, either exchanging referrals between you, or by them marketing your products or services for a commission.

- Repeat this exercise, this time looking at key suppliers in a *different* industry who have a relationship with your target clients, and where both you and they could benefit if you were to collaborate.

A different type of win-win relationship

When you're in business, if you don't have a partner working alongside you, you may have nobody close enough to the business to act as a sounding board and bounce ideas off. Many of the entrepreneurs we interviewed therefore utilized another form of outside assistance to help grow their ventures, in the form of business mentors, boards of advisors or professional coaches.

Having an external partner in the business (who has no financial ownership) enabled our entrepreneurs to get constructive input from specialists. Whether they were subject-matter experts (such as human resources, legal or finance) or specialized coaches, they challenged the entrepreneur to accelerate the growth of the business.

While the skills, experience and objectives of these groups of people were different, their objective was the same: to enable the entrepreneur to step outside of the day-to-day running of the business and look at the bigger picture of what they were doing, where they going and what they needed to focus on.

I have a mentor who runs a recruitment business as well. He's had experience of taking businesses to floatation and he provides valuable advice on how to grow my own business over regular breakfast meetings.

Jon Cuff, Cuff Jones

Before appointing an outside person it's worth considering what their credentials are. For instance, who else have they assisted, what was the outcome, and how much do they know about the operations of your specific industry? Depending on where you feel you are, you may benefit from a coach who will challenge to be your best but has no direct knowledge of your industry, or you may want someone who has been successful in your industry once before and has now moved on to a new challenge.

The appointment of an external specialist also provided another benefit to many of our entrepreneurs – when it came to opening new doors of possibility, the external person often came with their own little black book of contacts. While this would not be a reason on its own to hire them, it is something to consider when selecting the right person.

Getting external coaching has helped me understand where the edge of my competency is. When you're playing the game you can't watch yourself play, but if you have somebody on the outside watching the game they'll help show you how you're actually doing.

Peter Thomond, SportInspired

THINK ABOUT IT

Who within your network could act as your advisor? Is there somebody within your industry that many people look up to (either because of past achievements or present ones)?

Some people will charge for their services (that's their 'win'). Others may be generous enough to give you their advice for free, and derive satisfaction from passing on their experience. Whatever path you take, make sure you pick the right person to coach or mentor you.

IF YOU REMEMBER ONE THING

The people you have around you can help you grow your venture, whether it's reaching new clients through collaboration, or by helping you step outside of your venture and assess how well you and it are doing.

---

22. Achieving work–life balance

You can't punch out … you can't turn your phone off on vacation. You are never done as a small business.

Ryan Prettyman, Radiation Detection Services Inc.

During our research we asked entrepreneurs how they achieve a good work–life balance and the standard answer was to laugh and say, 'I don't'. Growing a venture is a little like nurturing a child. You create it, you are responsible for it, you care about it, it reflects on you and, most importantly, you can feel that you are *never* off duty.

Jon Cuff, Cuff Jones (launched 2010)
Having studied law and business at university and with a training contract lined up, Jon was approached and asked if he would consider working as a recruitment consultant in the legal industry. Excited by the opportunity to work within the legal field, but also to use the business knowledge that he had acquired during his degree, Jon took the role, a big decision at the time, but one that he has never regretted.

After six years of establishing himself and creating a strong reputation within the legal market, Jon decided that he wanted to set up his own recruitment firm. He discussed this decision with his then fiancée as working for himself would involve a temporary cut in pay, probably for around six months, while Jon established himself. Fortunately Jon's partner knew the industry herself, having worked in recruitment, and was very supportive of the venture. They named the business after both of their surnames, Cuff and Jones.

Jon took the plunge and for six months he was based from the table in his kitchen, getting on the books of clients he had previously worked with and speaking with candidates who were seeking new positions.

However, like many entrepreneurs starting up in tough economic times, Jon found it difficult to get his venture off the ground. This meant he had to be extremely dedicated to his work. For example, at the outset he could not afford to take on staff, so *every* phone call and *every* e-mail had to be answered by him personally. And he had to do a great job, in order to establish his reputation.

Here's an example of how this dedication translated into Jon's day-to-day life. He was anticipating a call from a client in an American-based firm to see if he was about to receive a placement offer for a candidate of his. The problem: Jon was in Buenos Aires at the time, where he was getting ready for his wedding. So while his fiancée was making the final preparations for the big day, Jon was pacing around the roof of the hotel, trying desperately to get a signal to find out whether the major deal was going to go through or not. This illustrates the extra mile that entrepreneurs must be prepared to go in order to succeed.

The good news is that Jon's work has paid off. He's already been able to hire two recruitment consultants to work for him, and is now looking to recruit a third. And best of all, his wife (and namesake of the business) has been able to join the business on a full-time basis. Now that the business has matured, there's cover and Jon has much needed back-up during critical moments. Plus it's a great adventure that he is now able to share and enjoy with his wife.

- What sacrifices are you willing to make in your personal life in order for your venture to succeed?

- Where do you draw the line?

This is me building for my future. However, with that comes a demand on your time and stress in your life.

Anna Hodgson, The Eternal Maker

Being an entrepreneur typically entails sacrifice

This book is not about sugarcoating the truth – entrepreneurs have to make sacrifices when growing their ventures. The story above is by no means the only one we've heard. The reality is that entrepreneurship can be a very unwanted intruder in your own life, which encroaches on the lives of your friends and family too.

One topic that came up regularly among the entrepreneurs we interviewed was the impact it had on their relationships. Many of them commented that it needed an understanding partner for them to be successful. Without that, slipping away from the dinner table to make an urgent phone call, or working on holiday, can mean that tensions occur. Jon was very fortunate that his partner was behind his venture, so it's important that your loved ones know and understand what your new working situation might entail.

What's critical is how you manage that sacrifice over the long-term. If you're not careful you can spend your whole time missing magic personal moments in your life, as you try and make the wheels of your venture turn. Yes, it's much more satisfying making your venture's wheels turn than an employer's, but even a fantastic venture isn't worth ruining the other parts of your life for. So how can you achieve a better balance?

Schedule time for the important things

If you are anything like our entrepreneurs, your venture is going to be one of the most important things in your life. You'll live it, breathe it and think about it virtually every day. As a result, your attention may not be on other areas of your life. It's therefore important to consciously set time aside to keep those plates spinning too.

An excellent piece of advice is to consider your friends,

family and relaxation time as your clients. When you plan how you will spend your time, consider scheduling in meetings with important people in your life. Imagine that they are one of your venture's most critical customers and only cancel your 'meeting' under extenuating circumstances. This will enable you to pay the time and attention to those other vital areas of your life, including physical health, mental well-being and close relationships, which in turn sustain you.

- Get next month's calendar in front of you.

- Who is important to you in your life? When would it be convenient to try and see them? Contact them and arrange a date now.

- What leisure activities would you like to do? Book time in your calendar for them.

Manage your clients' expectations

Many businesses have opening hours. If you walk past a store and you see a sign saying 'Open 24hrs' your immediate expectation is, rightly, that you can walk in any time of day and get served. However, if you know that a specialist store is closed after 6pm, your behaviour as a customer changes. You'll make sure you go to the specialist store before it closes because you can go to the 24hr store at any time.

Unless you manage your clients' expectations you risk

them becoming unreasonable. Remember, they want to do business with you because of the value and benefit you provide to them, so if you're on a date with your partner it's perfectly polite to say you'll call back at a convenient moment, especially if you give them a specific appointment time that you then deliver on. It also demonstrates that you're in demand from other people who value your time and energy (whether that's another client, or your golf buddy).

THINK ABOUT IT

- When clients think of your venture, what availability sign do they see connected to it?

- Is your answer to the above question the situation that you want, or do you need to manage their expectations better?

Manage your friends' and family's expectations

As well as thinking about the availability sign that you have for your clients, think about the availability sign that you have for your friends and family. We've found that it is helpful to politely remind well-meaning people that during working hours we are *working* and although we don't have a boss looking over our shoulder, that doesn't mean that we have time for long chats all day, or endless lunch breaks.

In some respects, when you are running your own venture it is even more important to work during your working hours (whatever they may be) or else you don't get paid. Work–life balance isn't just about achieving more of the 'life' aspect, it's about balancing two important demands on your time.

- When friends and family think of your venture, what availability sign do they see connected to it?

- Is your answer to the above question the situation that you want, or do you need to manage expectations better?

Use time-management techniques

Some of the other techniques that our entrepreneurs use to manage their time effectively include:

- **Batching e-mails**: Rather than being at the mercy of their inbox they allotted a certain time to review their e-mails, replying to any that needed it, then focusing on other commitments.

- **Setting deadlines**: When about to start something, setting a deadline for when you'll get it completed provides you with a target to aim for and helps you plan your time better.

- **Limiting face-to-face meetings**: At the beginning of a venture, being in front of a client is a good way to build trust within the relationship, but later on you could use your time more effectively by speaking over the phone instead.

Hire other people

When your venture has matured to a certain point, you may be able to bring in other people to help you use your time more effectively.

This doesn't have to be limited to people who you 'employ' in the traditional sense. A number of entrepreneurs have brought in administration assistants as a starting point; somebody who can just alleviate the time-consuming tasks that need to be done but don't require the owner to do them. In some cases these people have been part-time contractors, other times they have been remote, located overseas.

We'll cover more on employing people in the next chapter.

When you first start a business it's like a baby, like a child, you've got to give it 100 per cent. But when you bring people into the business, and you're paying them, in order to take the business to the next level you've got to have a little bit of work–life balance.

Tricia Topping, TTA Group

IF YOU REMEMBER ONE THING While you have a responsibility to grow and nurture your venture, you also have a responsibility to yourself and those who you value in your life. So put in place strategies that mean you can achieve a good balance between your personal and your entrepreneurial life.

23. Employing others

Yes, I'd recommend employing people when you've got money and when you can afford them. Try and recruit the best person you can work with.

Tricia Topping, TTA Group

It's fair to say that employing others can be one of the biggest headaches of your business. Employees come to work with their own potent mix of emotions, values, beliefs, concerns, motivations and needs. Plus, you may feel a weighty burden of responsibility if your employees rely on a salary from your business to pay their mortgages and feed their children. As the boss, it is your job to manage them and steer them in the right direction to ensure that everyone works as one team to deliver the goals of your business.

Some entrepreneurs see employing others as a hassle that isn't worth the pain. As a result, it isn't uncommon to hear solo entrepreneurs say that they never want to grow their business beyond themselves. Others reach a point – through choice or necessity – where they need extra manpower, either to deliver their core business or to take their ventures to the next level.

If you are at the stage where you are considering employing others, we recommend that you read two of our sister books in this series – *A Practical Guide to Leadership* and *A Practical Guide to Management*. These titles will give you an in-depth and practical guide to delivering business objectives to others.

This chapter focuses on one message that came out especially loud and clear during our entrepreneurship research. That message was this: when you own a venture, and you need or want others to deliver on your behalf, you have to create a win-win relationship with your staff. Here's an example of the rewards that this can reap.

Susan Heavilin, MicroTest, Inc. (launched in 1984)

Susan and her husband started a small business in the garage of their home in Phoenix, Arizona with an investment of $10,000. Less than ten years later, it had gone public on NASDAQ, employing 500 people across its headquarters in Phoenix and international offices in the UK and The Hague.

From interviewing Susan, it is clear that there were two key factors behind her company's success: their product and their attitude towards staff.

To begin with, the company had created a new niche with an innovative product. With the increase of computers in the 1980s, there was a desire to connect office computers using Local Area Networks (LANs). MicroTest would set up the LANs, installing computer network cabling into the ceilings, but because the cabling technology was so unreliable at that time, after just a couple of weeks it could develop a problem and cause the entire system to go down. Because the network was embedded in the ceiling it was almost impossible to fix or locate the problem. Susan came up with an idea for a handheld device that would connect to the computer cable, diagnose the fault and pinpoint where it was located.

Although it was very expensive to make a prototype of the device, the effort was worth it. The next step was to demonstrate the 'Cable Scanner' at the 'must-attend' COMDEX trade show in Las Vegas. A display booth was built in their driveway and transported by truck to the trade show. The Cable Scanner, a product well ahead of its time, was the hit of COMDEX that year and the queue to see it was wrapped around the building.

Their new product gave birth to almost 30 new products and made MicroTest a leading producer of network test and connectivity products.

Susan and her husband had created a niche that had never existed before and word spread, generating so much demand that they couldn't possibly produce enough to be able to supply everybody. From large companies like Exxon through to the White House, there was widespread demand for the Cable Scanner. This huge demand led to a need to hire a number of people, including more engineers, marketing and salespeople. And this is where Susan and her partner's attitude towards staff became the second major asset of their business.

'A lot of people who have a company take lots of money from it and buy expensive cars, houses and boats. We never did that. The people who worked for us earned more money than we did – we put everything back into the company and it just grew and grew. We would have a big party each Christmas and would give people big bonuses.'

Susan is a strong advocate that you need to empower employees to succeed in business. She chose not to treat them as employees, but to treat everyone as equals. The ethos was that everyone worked together as a team, like a big family. The more the organization sold, the more everyone got back.

Susan believes that it is essential to reward your employees richly, with a good compensation of company stock or through generous bonuses. You should find some way to reward your employees for their efforts because they are important to the success of your company and you can't do it without them. Although Susan and her husband had a great product, this was nothing without the dedicated team who worked with them.

As testament to the success of the product and the people, MicroTest, Inc. was acquired by competitor Fluke Networks in 2001 and was sold on NASDAQ for approximately $74 million. Not bad for a business started in a garage!

I think it's really important to take care of the
people who take care of your business.

Steve Rosko, So Cal TTC

Getting the best from employing others

Our services have recently been hired by a major UK organization to help them understand what aspects of leadership drive excellent customer service within highly successful organizations. We studied many different global companies who are renowned for customer excellence, with several key themes emerging from our research:

1. There is a link between motivated, happy staff and business profitability.

2. In successful organizations, the whole business is aligned behind a common goal, and works together as 'one team'.

3. Successful organizations with great customer service reward their staff richly, for example through generous profit-sharing schemes.

4. Successful organizations with great customer service really look after the welfare of their staff. They take the view that if you look after your staff, they will look after your business's customers.

As we interviewed Susan, these themes really resonated with what she was saying.

*Always treat your employees exactly as you
want them to treat your best customers.*

Stephen Covey, author

Who should I hire?

The following questions should guide your thinking during
the hiring process.

What support do I need?

In order for you to realize the value in employing others it's
important to be clear as to what your needs are. Does your
venture need somebody to drive sales, deliver products,
innovate new products, or put in place your operations?
Being clear on what your venture's needs are at any one
time improves the chances of hiring the right person.

One of our entrepreneurs took an interesting approach
to this question. He hired people into the business that were
critical for core operations: sales and product delivery. But
he simultaneously utilizes their whole skillset to support the
operational side of the business, something which is part
of the culture of the organization and people are happy
to do. When there's a problem with IT, one of his staff is
capable of fixing it, which means that an IT person doesn't
yet have to be employed on a full-time basis (which isn't
needed at this stage). It also avoids the need to bring in
costly IT consultants, as the problem can be fixed in-house.
Note however that as your venture grows, you'll probably
want to employ people in more specialist functions.

What attributes should I hire for?

You'll need to consider what it is about the person coming on board that your venture will value most. Is it their experience, competence, attitude, or qualifications? It may be best to think through each of these attributes and decide which are 'essential' for the role and which are 'desirable'. Interestingly, during our research into customer service excellence, another message that came through loud and clear was that you should hire for attitude. You can teach skills, but you can't teach people a positive attitude. Plus if people have a positive attitude, they are more likely to be flexible and to adopt a one-team mindset, which means you can utilize their skillset more diversely if needed.

What employment basis should I choose?

Our research has found that young ventures often prefer to have more flexible arrangements, while those that are more established have more permanent ones. Newer ventures don't confine themselves to the traditional 'full time, employed, based at my premises' model. For instance, some entrepreneurs use freelancers who act as long-term associates for their business, typically on a 'zero-hour' basis, meaning that the venture didn't promise them any fixed amount of income but ensured that there was a network of a team in place who could be called upon when required. Those freelancers who worked with clients typically had a non-compete clause in their agreements, which was fair to both parties and protected the venture from the risk of losing its clients to its associates.

This proved to be a real win-win relationship: the freelancers benefited from having an entrepreneur feeding their business when there was demand (therefore avoiding the need to do sales and marketing themselves); the entrepreneur benefited from having a remote team who could be called upon to represent them when needed. Plus the remote team could be featured on their website, making their organization appear larger.

 If you are considering taking staff on board, take the opportunity now to answer the following questions to assess how to find the right candidate:

- What is it your venture needs to retain its current clients and gain further ones?

- What are the essential attributes that a person has to have to deliver on the needs you've identified?

- What are the desirable attributes that person needs?

- Looking over the ways to employ somebody, which will offer you the greatest value when compared to the risk and the cost of employing somebody?

Remember that you can find more information on how to hire people in our sister book in this series, *A Practical Guide to Management*.

When looking to employ someone in any capacity, it's important to consider the employment law in the country where they're employed, getting specialist advice where necessary. Employment law will impact what arrangements you need to have in place when hiring someone and the rights they have before, during and after their employment with you.

Bringing employees into your venture can mean that your venture grows faster and better. While the costs of employing somebody can be a factor, the right person employed in the right way for what your venture needs means that their value can far exceed that.

24. Serial entrepreneurship

I built up those other business to the point where they were running themselves, but rather than sell them, kept them on. Providing you have the right people and managers for the day-to-day it can work.

Sarah Hodgson, The Button Company

So far this book has concentrated on finding a niche and then expanding your business into complementary areas. However, some entrepreneurs, for example Richard Branson, have grown their business portfolio through the acquisition of ventures in radically different industries to their initial enterprise.

This chapter looks at how seasoned entrepreneurs expand their interests into different businesses and explores their ingenuity in the face of challenge.

Sarah Hodgson, The Button Company (purchased in 2000)

Sarah was deeply saddened by the decline of British manufacturing, an industry that put the 'great' into Great Britain back in the 19th century. Inspired by a passion to keep British manufacturing alive, Sarah decided to fight for it and purchased a failing button factory, including taking on the financial burden of a four-year lease and six staff. This was somewhat of a bold move as, at the time, Sarah knew *nothing* about button manufacturing!

However, Sarah was already an experienced entrepreneur, and this stood her in good stead to turn the ailing factory around. She already had a diverse and profitable business portfolio that she had built up, including, among others, one that imported and distributed loft ladders and staircases, and a manufacturing business for chimney terminals (cowls, flues and other fireplace products).

Sarah's entrepreneurial skills, coupled with ownership of her other profitable ventures, meant that she was well placed to take on the ailing factory without unacceptable risk to her own livelihood or the rest of her portfolio.

Sarah used her expertise to make the button factory profitable once again. However, four years later, with a healthy turnaround under her belt, disaster struck, when Sarah's industry changed overnight. Restrictions on trading Chinese fabric were lifted and the UK garment industry was destroyed, taking The Button Company's core client base with it. Because there was nobody to sell buttons to anymore, they had to stop manufacturing them and the factory closed. Customers returned the unused stocks they had and Sarah had a mountain of buttons left over.

And then the true spirit of entrepreneurship was shown. A phoenix can rise from the ashes.

Having closed the factory, Sarah needed much smaller premises to store the button mountain, and the most suitable location at the time happened to be the storeroom of a local retail outlet. Although Sarah didn't need the shop front, it gave her an interesting idea – she could offer the shop to her daughter who could run it as a craft business and sell the button mountain as a result. In other words Sarah could use her assets (the buttons and unwanted shop floor space) and offer them to a new target market (retail crafters). This market was far less impacted by the change in trading restrictions and this gave Sarah's daughter a great opportunity in the process.

This was an excellent win-win solution and Anna Hodgson's business, The Eternal Maker – featured in Chapter 5 – was born.

And Sarah never gave up on her dream of fighting for British manufacturing. Over the last couple of years the UK has experienced a new trend – a surge in appetite for quality goods that are authentically 'Made In Britain'. Sarah has recently decided to get the machines firing again and restart production for this growing niche.

In the 1990s there were 30 active polyester button factories in the UK; now The Button Company is the last. It seems as if Sarah really is achieving her dream of keeping British manufacturing alive. Such is the power of entrepreneurship!

When you've grown up with parents who are entrepreneurs, setting up a business is not such a big step. You've seen the highs, you've seen the lows, so it's no big deal.

Anna Hodgson, The Eternal Maker

How could you use your entrepreneurial skills to make a difference, either to other aspiring entrepreneurs or to industries you feel passionate about?

Minimize the downsides of risk

Richard Branson has commented that 'minimizing the downsides of risk' is one of the most important phrases in his life. When making bold moves, such as taking on an ailing venture you know nothing about, you need to ensure that there is a way out if something goes wrong.

This attitude was illustrated in Branson's approach to transitioning from the music business to setting up an airline. When launching Virgin Atlantic, Branson leased a plane from Boeing that could be returned after twelve months if the business wasn't successful enough. Critically, this meant that if the venture failed, it would not bring down the rest of his business. Branson was quite clear that he did not want people in his music company to lose their jobs from a failed branch-out initiative.

This approach to business reflects the ethos of this whole book, which was summarized in the introduction. Being an entrepreneur may *appear* risky to others; however, successful entrepreneurs manage that risk and protect the downsides of it.

Making your ventures run themselves

There's another key factor that supports serial entrepreneurship (and a better work–life balance) and that is building up your ventures to a point where they run themselves so that you no longer need to be involved on a day-to-day basis.

For example, Sarah has structured her other businesses so that the staff within the company make day-to-day operating decisions, while she only gets involved in anything outside of this, such as strategic decision-making. Because she has taken those businesses to the next level and they can run themselves, this means that she only needs to spend half a day a week on those at maximum. This enabled Sarah to devote her time to The Button Company when it needed her most.

For a number of our entrepreneurs, not having to be 100 per cent involved day-to-day is a key milestone which they are/were aiming for. It means delegating responsibilities to those around them, whether it be decision-making to a manager, financial management to the accountant, production to contractors, or sales duties to their staff. As long as the plates could keep spinning without them needing to have a hand on every one of them, the venture carried its own momentum.

Returning to our analogy of an entrepreneurial venture being like a child, some of our entrepreneurs are aiming to grow their businesses to a point where they no longer need 'parental supervision' all of the time, freeing them up for other opportunities.

THINK ABOUT IT Imagine how you would feel about your venture if you suddenly got the urge to go on vacation for a month and travel around a different part of the world. Would you be able to leave your venture running successfully without you present?

- Write down all of the responsibilities or tasks that you have had to do as an entrepreneur.

- Beside each of them, rank them on a scale of 1–10 (1 = low, 10 = high) of how critical it is to the venture that you are the one who does them.

- For anything that is less than an 8, write down who you can empower with this responsibility that is already available to you. If there is no one you can currently trust to do it, consider how you can empower a person in the future to take this responsibility (e.g. training people up, recruiting somebody, outsourcing it).

- For anything that is 8 or above, consider whether you can involve others in part of what you absolutely have to keep yourself – so that they get experience of doing it and freeing up some more of your time – without them taking over full responsibility for it.

IF YOU REMEMBER ONE THING Once you have a successful venture up and running you may want to consider applying your entrepreneurship skills by expanding your portfolio into new markets with new ventures and ensuring you have the right staff to keep the original enterprise going in your absence.

25. New horizons

I think about what's next for me because I have lots of other interests. When I'm truly happy with what I've done here, and when I think I can no longer grow, that's as a coach or as a business, it'll be time to consider something new.

Steve Rosko, So Cal TTC

Throughout this book we've seen how embarking on an entrepreneurial venture can be a bit like having a child. Ventures and babies can sometimes be hard to conceive, and once born they require a lot of hard work. As they grow older, they gain increasing capability to act independently without constant supervision, until one day, you are no longer needed on a day-to-day basis. When that 'young adult' is ready to leave home for the first time, the parent and the entrepreneur must both decide what to focus their energies on next.

Your venture at a crossroads

Once your venture has become established, you are likely to find yourself at a crossroads where there are a number of options available. For example, you could:

- Carry on as before, with you at the helm, and heavily involved in day-to-day operations.

- Stay at the helm and step back to let someone else manage the enterprise on a daily basis, but still retain overall responsibility for the venture.

- Pass the reins on, and devolve your responsibility as a result, but still remain involved in an advisory capacity or for public relations purposes, for example by occupying a 'Chairman' role.

- Sell it to another organization and remain in the enterprise in a position agreed with the new owner.

- Sell it to another organization and leave the enterprise.

- Close it – it may be that the venture has run its course, or that none of the other options are available, so you decide to wind it down.

Each option will need to be explored in terms of financial and practical viability, including whether it works for your needs as well as the needs of your venture's stakeholders (e.g. employees, clients, suppliers).

In the following case study, we'll see how an entrepreneurial journey encompassed a number of these options over the course of time.

Tricia Topping, TTA Group (launched 1989)
Tricia has always had a passion for entrepreneurship. Even during her early career she succeeded in building and selling a cosmetics company. In the late 1980s, with the 'entrepreneurial bug' still in her, Tricia spotted a gap in the market for a public relations (PR) company that specialized in the property industry.

Tricia therefore made the decision to begin the journey of launching a business within this niche.

Although Tricia already had a wealth of entrepreneurial experience under her belt, she wanted to learn the ropes of the PR industry. She sought and attained a PR Account Executive role in a London-based PR company. Eighteen months later, with some useful contacts and some helpful PR skills and experience under her belt, Tricia was ready to launch her own consultancy – Tricia Topping Associates (TTA).

Over the next fourteen years, Tricia grew her privately owned company, employing a team of people and picking up numerous awards and prestigious clients along the way. Tricia's vision was realized – she had become a dominant player in the PR industry.

Tricia's plan was always to sell her consultancy firm, a goal that was achieved in 2003, when 70 per cent of Tricia's company was acquired by a major global PR consultancy. Tricia's brand and leadership was strong, and therefore even though her business was part-owned by the parent organization, it continued to be known by the brand name 'TTA' and Tricia continued to work as Chief Executive.

This role was not without challenges. Tricia had to lead her business through tough economic conditions, with responsibilities to staff and shareholders, and the additional test of working for a public company. Yet it is testament to the working relationship between Tricia and her employers and colleagues that she stayed at the helm for another decade.

But Tricia is the first to admit that achievement is not without its sacrifice. Numerous early starts and late nights at work equated to losing precious time with friends and family, a strain on health and missing out on the simple pleasures in life. So in 2012, Tricia decided to pass over the reins of responsibility into capable hands and assumed a Chairman role in the organization. She now acts as an ambassador for the company, maintaining good relations with clients, generating new business and promoting the group.

Although it can be very hard to let go of something that you've grown and for which you've been responsible for many years, the decision to move on can bring a welcome new lease of life. Tricia now has the best of both worlds – she's no longer under the same degree of pressure as when she was the Chief Executive of the business, yet she's still actively involved and can still contribute to its success – a bit like being a grandparent to the business. Plus she also has more time in her life for hobbies that she previously overlooked, such as playing golf. Tricia is proud of the journey she's been on, but is also pleased to have begun a new chapter in her life.

A new chapter begins

Your venture by this point probably feels like a real family member. Something that has taken such love, attention and dedication to get to where it is will undoubtedly invoke some emotions whatever decision is taken. To assist you in considering what your venture's next steps are let's take a look at where this journey began.

End with the beginning in mind

At the outset we told you that we advocate *beginning with the end in mind*. When it comes to a crossroads and the possible end of your time with your venture, it's important to reconsider what we covered in the beginning of this book: the 'MAP to Success'. Let's consider how your venture has evolved compared to that map:

M – Meaning

- Is your venture still giving you a sense of meaning?

- Is it accomplishing the values you hold most dear?

- Or is it still giving you the opportunity to pursue meaning elsewhere?

A – Achievement

- Have you achieved what you set out to?

- Are you satisfied with the accomplishments that you have made?

- Are there further challenges that your venture could pursue that excite you?

P – Positive Emotions

- Do you still feel good about your venture?

- Do you enjoy working within your venture?

- Is your venture contributing to a net positive experience in your life?

In other words, through your entrepreneurial venture, are you still:

*Experiencing **positive emotions** and **meaning** in life whilst striving to **achieve** your entrepreneurial goals?*

- Go ahead and answer the questions we've posed above in relation to your venture.

- Is there something new and exciting that you want to try? Has there been something you just can't stop thinking about doing, and is now the time to commit to doing it?

Be honest with your answers, even if they're not the answers you'd like. Every entrepreneur will at some stage have to consider these when at a crossroads – it doesn't commit you to a decision, it just helps shine the light on what your venture is contributing to your life.

IF YOU REMEMBER ONE THING The value that an entrepreneur creates should be celebrated. Often, it is reflected in the legacy that they leave behind. Successful entrepreneurs create jobs, transform industries, enhance societies and change lives. Plus they inspire people along the way. This is all part of the legacy you will be contributing to during your time as an entrepreneur.

A huge number of people that I've trained have now gone on to be managing directors elsewhere. They come back to me and thank me. They still have reunions to discuss the days when they worked together. Knowing that's the impact I've had, that I'm responsible for such strong relationships, that's been the most rewarding part of it all.

Tricia Topping, TTA Group

Consider the impact that the entrepreneurs featured in this book have had. You've already learned that Sarah Hodgson (The Button Company owner) and Anna Hodgson (owner of The Eternal Maker) are mother and daughter. We haven't yet told you that Martin Stephenson (the owner of Hunts County Bats) is the proud father of Richard, featured in Chapter 2, who led The Westminster Challenge on its Arctic expedition. Plus Tricia Topping was Alison's first ever boss, Alison having worked at TTA after graduating from university. As an entrepreneur, you never know who, or what you will inspire.

We wish you every success on the rest of your entrepreneurial journey.

Acknowledgements

We would like to thank all of those entrepreneurs who told us their stories and agreed to share them with you. They are listed below in the order of their case study appearance in this book:

Peter Thomond and Richard Raynes, SportInspired
　www.sportinspired.org
Richard Stephenson
Deon Girdhar and Chris Williams, Zay D Entertainment
　www.zay-d.com
Steve Roe, Hoopla
　www.hooplaimpro.com
Anna Hodgson, The Eternal Maker
　www.eternalmaker.com
Richard Copsey and Kate Smith, Holtwhites Bakery
　www.holtwhitesbakery.co.uk
Andrew Gittins, Proposal Automation
　www.proposalautomation.co.uk
Steve Rosko, So Cal TTC
　www.so-calttc.com
Beverley Christie, Beauty Sensation
　www.beautysensation.co.uk
Ryan Prettyman, Radiation Detection Services Inc.
　www.radiationds.com
Dianna Bonner, World Vision Photos
　www.worldvisionphotos.co.uk

Facebook.com/Dianna.Bonner.Photographer
Twitter.com/DiannaBonner
Cémanthe Harris, New Media Angels
www.newmediaangels.com
Martin Stephenson, Hunts County Bats
www.huntscountybats.co.uk
Andy Carley, Response Development Training
www.responsedt.com
Jon Cuff, Cuff Jones
www.cuffjones.com
Susan Heavilin
Sarah Hodgson, The Button Company
www.buttoncompany.co.uk
Tricia Topping, TTA Group
www.ttagroup.co.uk

Index